# ADVANCED

## MOUNTAIN FLYING TECHNIQUES

DAVID HOERNER

2005

Cover photograph taken by: Derrick Reich

Disclaimer:

The techniques described in this manual have been learned and used during thousands of hours of flying in the mountains. The author doesn't in any way imply that his techniques are the only way to fly in the mountains. Using these techniques doesn't guarantee that a pilot will not find himself in life-threatening situations or survive life-threatening situations. Pilots should use this manual only as a guideline to help them in their endeavor to be better mountain pilots. Each pilot is responsible for his/her decisions when flying, and must develop his/her own system and techniques. Flying and being safe in the mountains is the full responsibility of each pilot and not the author of this manual.

# ADVANCED

## MOUNTAIN FLYING TECHNIQUES

ACKNOWLEDGEMENTS:

Special thanks to Sarah for spending hours getting the manual prepared for the publisher and to Sarah and Linda for their excellent editing. Thanks also to Susan for communicating with the publisher and getting the job done.

Thank you to Derrick Reich for taking the cover photo.

# DEDICATION:

This book is dedicated to my children, Ryan and Bree. Both of them are the pride of my life. Ryan stood tall, looked you in the eyes, and held his hand out with a big smile. He was one hell of a mountain pilot and my best friend. Even though he is not with us now, his memory will live on forever.

# TABLE OF CONTENTS:

# CHAPTER 1:

# BEING PREPARED

All types of flying involve risk, **but mountain flying creates added risk that needs to be considered before you commit yourself and your family to life-threatening situations.** Mountain flying is not an exact science, and no one can say there is only one way to fly in the mountains. There are different theories and approaches, but all pilots need to learn safe, proven techniques from those who have experience in this treacherous terrain.

I have used the techniques described in this advanced mountain training manual for thousands of flight hours in the steep and windswept Rocky Mountains. All of these techniques have been learned from real life experiences. My goal is to help pilots understand the dangers associated with mountain flying, not to sell books. None of these techniques were thought up while sitting at a desk, but learned from actual, and at times scary, flights. Hopefully this manual will help pilots understand mountain weather and give them a basic knowledge to help them make good decisions while flying in the mountains.

If you study the information in this manual, and **follow the *Twenty Rules to Live By*, your chance of getting into a dangerous situation will diminish drastically.** Use these rules as your guide to stay alive.

Once you have absorbed the information in this manual your fear of the unknown or basic techniques about flying in mountainous terrain will be gone. Armed with this, a safe mountain flight is possible with the rewards of aqua-blue mountain lakes, crystal clear waterfalls, and sparkling white glaciers unattainable while land-bound.

Hopefully you will gain a healthy respect for the mountains. You will know what can happen, where to fly, and most importantly how to read the weather. Your mind will feel at ease and you will gain confidence, resulting in a pleasurable mountain flight.

This book is written for anyone who will be flying over or around mountainous terrain. It doesn't matter if you're a fledgling student pilot or an experienced airline captain. Flying over and around steep mountain peaks or rolling mountains can be scary and demanding.

This book is a guideline to help you fly in mountains safely, but basic flying skills are assumed and won't be covered. You already know how to fly or will when you get your license. Through the following chapters we will discuss in detail the following items:

1. Be prepared. Part of being prepared is knowing your abilities. What is the weather? What are the best routes? Is the airplane capable of handling your route? Is the pilot in the right state of mind?
2. Engine failures with a dead-stick landing and decisions made from the first sign of the problem. What are the right and wrong procedures while handling an emergency.
3. Mountain flying techniques with emphasis on winds; discussion on turbulence, downdrafts, ridge flying, and wind shear.

4. Knowing where to fly. Choosing the best routes to fly when the wind is blowing.
5. Death in Glacier Park. This chapter will discuss the decisions made and the disastrous end of pushing the weather in some of the steepest and most dangerous terrain in the United States.
6. Weather. Includes scud running and when to turn back.
7. Landing and takeoff techniques on high mountain airstrips: the best known techniques for approaching, landing at, and departing from mountain airstrips.
8. Unimproved runways, off-airport and emergency landings.
9. Emergency survival gear.
10. Mountain Flying Airplanes, including a discussion on which airplanes handle the mountains and which ones are marginal and various mechanical problems.

**Pilots who have flown into the mountains unprepared for the demanding flight conditions have been injured and killed, or at the very least, scared.** We need to ask ourselves truthfully, am I getting into a situation I can't handle? Am I prepared for the wind and weather?

Do I have enough **understanding and knowledge** of mountain flying techniques?

You purchased this manual to better prepare yourself. That's the first step, wanting to be prepared, so let's get started and conquer the mountains!

At times all pilots sit on the ground. It doesn't matter how much experience he/she may have, safety demands waiting for better conditions. Mother Nature is unpredictable and a lot stronger than any airplane or human attitude. Pilots need to tread lightly with what they can't control and use sound reasoning formulated from strong information.

On a bone-shaking windy day, choosing where to fly is paramount. Changing your flight path by just a few hundred feet can make a dangerous flight more comfortable—and possible. **The bottom line: knowing when to go, where to fly, when to turn around, and when to pushing the weather can save your life.**

The next nine chapters will prepare you to know the answers to these questions. Of course, our own mistakes leave the most lasting impression, but learning from another pilot's experiences is certainly the easier and safer approach. We will scrutinize a couple of airplane wrecks (or near-wrecks) made by other pilots and try to understand what led to the accident and learn what not to do.

Wind can be the hardest element to understand, in part because it is invisible. A knowledgeable mountain pilot usually has an idea of wind direction and speed. The last thing a mountain pilot wants to do is fly into a 50 mile-an-hour downdraft wind. **The turbulence created**

**by that type of wind could cause structural damage to the aircraft, or even worse, cause the pilot to lose control.** Usually Mother Nature gives clues about what the wind is doing. Pilots need to pay close attention to these clues.

As seen in the picture to the left, **lenticular clouds warn of high winds, the height of the winds, and their direction.** One glance should warn a pilot where not to fly and how to avoid them. Moisture-laden air is forced up from a lower level in the valley. The temperature drops, causing the air to increase in speed and condense into a visual cloud. This cloud over the mountain indicates high wind, which in turn means turbulent air.

Other clues to look for are leaves or trees. If you're flying close enough to see which direction the limbs or leaves are blowing, it shows the direction of the wind. The bottom side of leaves usually have a lighter color. If the lighter-colored side is showing, it is pointing downwind.

High mountain lakes usually will be calm on the upwind side of the lake and be wavy downwind due to wind friction as the wind blows across the lake. Smoke, and even a herd of elk standing on an open ridge with their butts facing into the wind indicate wind direction.

Clouds, fog, or visible moisture do not pose an immediate danger, but mountain winds do because you can't see the wind. If the pilot looks out the window and sees the clouds lowering it should give him/her time to turn around and retreat to the nearest airport.

One very important point to remember is if an airplane is flown in the right location, **the same dangerous wind can be turned into a friend that lifts your airplane and propels you forward providing a smooth ride.** Knowing where to fly is paramount.

No mountain pilot takes off without a plan to fly the safest route and smoothest air possible. Flying in the mountains is dangerous enough. Then add turbulent air rolling off the backside of a ridge and the danger factor drastically rises.

We have all heard stories of flatland pilots that crashed into a rising terrain or tried to fly down a fog-shrouded valley only to fly into instrument conditions with the end result being tragic to the passenger's and pilot's family. Personally, I dislike flying over the flatlands without the mountains to use as a visual guide. These conditions force me to use my trusty vary omni range (VOR) or automatic direction finder (ADF).

The global positioning satellite (GPS) helps navigating in the flatlands. Some of the newer GPS's have moving maps with a topo display, making navigating in the mountains much easier. It's not mandatory to have a moving map GPS, but it sure lessens the work load when flying in limited visibility.

In the mountains, landmarks such as peaks, canyons, and ridges help keep track of your direction of flight, or which valley you're in. This is important to know when you are trying to find lower terrain if the weather is deteriorating.

Three questions to remember while flying in mountainous terrain are: what are the winds doing, what is the cloud cover, and what is the visibility? If conditions aren't right for your mountain flying skills and knowledge, then change your schedule. **The first *Rule to Live By* is: BE PREPARED.** Being prepared means you know the weather, know your capabilities, and know your aircraft's performance.

I've spent the last twenty years acquiring over 25,000 hours of flight time in the Rocky Mountains locating thousands of animals for the government. During these low-level flights I have encountered every conceivable adverse weather condition and have managed to stay alive. Believe me when I say, "I've had my share of close calls." I always took the time to think about what I'd done poorly and how I could have avoided the problem.

One very important item I learned was that it doesn't matter how much mountain experience you have, there are times when you must wait for the weather to improve. With that thought in mind, **the second** *Rule to Live By* is: IF CAUTION ISN'T USED, PEOPLE CAN GET HURT.

Always be ready to change your flight route. Never let a bad situation deteriorate to the point it's too late to get out of trouble. If you're not sure, turn back while you still have time.

The past 20 years have had their share of dangerous moments. I survived five engine failures and three dead-stick landings. I was lucky to be in the right location to find a survivable landing spot on each occasion. These potentially life-threatening problems remain etched firmly in my memory, and you can benefit from my experience.

Engine gauges, such as oil pressure and manifold pressure, indicate the health of your aircraft's engines. **If either gauge's indicator needle fluctuates abruptly**, you probably have the beginning of an engine problem. Turn back immediately before the problem turns into a situation that can't be handled by even the most experienced pilot.

My son, Ryan, and I recently bought a Cessna 182 in Chicago and were flying back to Montana. The oil pressure gauge fluctuated constantly. The plane had been burning or leaking over a quart of oil per hour. The needle slowly moved to the bottom of the green arc. We had a problem. We guessed there was a problem with rings or valves in the engine. Altitude is safety so we  climbed to twelve thousand feet elevation where Ryan leveled the plane.

We were directly over the Seely Lake airport. The indicator needle lowered to near zero.

I then had Ryan put the plane in a nose high attitude, the oil pressure climbed back into the green arc. This indication told me the problem: we were low on oil. When the plane was put in a climb, the oil flowed to the back of the oil pan, where the sump is located. The oil pump had more oil to pump with the nose-high attitude, which in turn created more pressure. When Ryan leveled the plane at twelve, the oil flowed forward in the oil pan, making less oil at the sump and decreasing pressure.

Since we were directly over the runway, we shut the engine off and circled down to land. The engine had only three quarts of oil. Tearing down the engine revealed broken rings which let the oil pass by the rings and then pumped overboard. **Pay close attention to your gauges. Any abrupt or unusual movement of the needles in the gauges could be an indication of a serious problem.**

In this first chapter we have discussed some important items and learned the first two *Rules to Live By*. Keep this book handy. In the back is a checklist you can use to refresh your memory and confirm you have planned well before flying in mountains. After a few flights the mountain flying techniques you have learned in this book will be part of your growing knowledge of flying.

CHAPTER 1 QUESTIONS:

1. What four questions does a pilot need to be able to answer while flying in the mountains?

   _____

   _____

   _____

2. Flying into fifty mile-an-hour downdraft winds can cause what to happen to a pilot?

   _____

   _____

3. What will lenticular clouds warn a pilot of?

   _____

   _____

4. Leaves blowing in a tree can tell a pilot what?

   _____

   _____

5. Why aren't clouds, fog, or visible moisture an immediate danger to a pilot? _____

   _____

6. Unseen mountain winds can have what effect on an airplane?

   _____

   _____

7. If an airplane is flown in the right location, what can be the results?

   _____

   _____

8. If weather in the mountains exceeds a pilot's skills, what should the pilot do?_____

9. What is the first *Rule to Live By* and explain its meaning.

   _____

   _____

10. What is the second *Rule to Live By* and explain its meaning.

    _____

    _____

11. If an engine pressure gauge fluctuates abruptly, what is probably happening?_____

    _____

    _____

# CHAPTER 2:

# DEAD STICK LANDING

John Vore, a Montana biologist, and I flew into the South Fork of the Flathead River counting elk for the government. The study area is thirty miles east of Kalispell over the Swan Mountains at the upper end of Hungry Horse Reservoir and in the Bob Marshall Wilderness. The Continental Divide runs the full length of the wilderness with mountains over 10,000 feet. Dense forests cover the first half of the mountain sides and rocky steep peaks rise above the tree line. There aren't many, if any, places to make an emergency landing in this area.

The elk thrive in this wilderness environment and stared at the Cessna 185. After a couple of flights, the elk showed little fear of the loud bird invading their space. For an added bonus, we would get an occasional glimpse of a wolf pack. On this flight I didn't have my skis on the plane; a big mistake. The skis would make it possible to land in any open area and remain upright. The possibility of an engine failure always remained in the back of my mind.

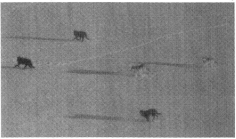

This remote area is a great place to spend some free time in the summer, but in the winter it is a different story. Snow piles three feet deep making landing without skis impossible. If I had attempted to land in the deep snow, the wheels would dig in until the added drag would force the plane to flip over onto its back. Deep snow might as well be water; any attempt to land would end in a crash landing. I was upset with myself for not taking the time to put the skis on. The sound of the smooth running engine offered some comfort, but the thought of mechanical problem lingered.

There are two airstrips in the area: Spotted Bear and Meadow Creek. Each has sufficient length for landing and departing and both have good approaches. The clear, gin-colored water invites relaxation and the urge to catch a fish during the summer months. It's a favorite spot for many local pilots. The deep canyons around these airstrips can cause the summer air to become turbulent in the heat of the afternoon. **To avoid high density altitudes and turbulent air, it is wise to leave similar airstrips early in the day**.

We dived, circled, and slid around trees. It was necessary to get close to the elk since they needed classification. We could identify bulls by their horns or lighter coloration. The difference between young and old can be determined by the length of their noses, and calves resemble cows except for their size.

As we counted herd after herd we slowly flew north from the South Fork to the Middle Fork of the Flathead River. The mountains rise 8,000 feet with the lower half covered with heavy spruce and fir timber, and the upper half with grassy open areas and steep, rocky mountain tops.

The pressure of mechanical problems eased as we crossed the high peaks of the Great Bear Wilderness and floated down to lower elevations in the Middle Fork drainage. Highway 2 extends the full length of the drainage, and has plenty of straight stretches suitable for an emergency landing. Glad to find the last herd of elk and finish the count, all we wanted was to return to the office, have a steaming cup of coffee, and recover from the motion of the flight.

The fastest route back would be to fly southwest over the Great Bear Wilderness. I'd spent thousands of hours flying over this area and knew it like the back of my hand. I also knew that having engine problems in this area would be disastrous.

The other option was to follow the highway down the drainage. Eventually, it would lead us to the Flathead Valley and into Kalispell. This route is fifteen minutes longer than the first, but had the safety of a highway all the way to town. The question was: **over the mountains or down the highway?** I hesitated briefly as both routes buzzed through my mind.

**Taking the safe route should have been my immediate decision,** but back then I still had a lot to learn. Justifying the risk, I reasoned I was tired, and it would be smoother and faster over the top. The sooner I got to Kalispell, the sooner I could get a cup of coffee. In hindsight, all my reasons were pretty lame.

What was I thinking? I was getting paid by the hour! So we followed the highway. We bounced down the drainage, with the high mountains lining each side of our route. The occasional glimpse of the highway below made for a care-free flight. I zigzagged, hunting for smooth air. One more sharp turn brought us out of the mountains and into the foothills of the Flathead Valley. We were home free. Well, just about.

A slight increase in the familiar vibration in the control yoke caused a moment of doubt as I stared at the engine instruments to see if I had imagined something wrong. Having flown thousands of hours in this 185, I knew its every characteristic. My gut told me something was different, even though everything appeared normal.

The subtle vibration grew in intensity until I knew there was a problem. I scanned the gauges to seek out the cause of the vibration. They didn't help, everything was in the green. The vibration turned to a shake. There was no doubt now. I had a problem that was turning into an emergency.

Without hesitation, I turned toward the highway. Instantly, the control yoke started oscillating in my hand, forcing me to grab hold with both hands. A second later a big bang in the engine compartment confirmed what I already knew was about to happen - an engine failure.

RPMs fell to eighteen hundred as I added power to compensate. I glanced to see if I would make it to the highway. **On top of the engine cowling was a new lump protruding upward.** One of the cylinders must have broken loose and slammed into the cowling.

The plane shook as the engine vibrated, forcing me to pull the power to an idle or lose the engine completely. The vibration grew in intensity. I knew the engine mounts wouldn't hold up to the abuse much longer. I pulled the mixture control out to the stop, and the vibration slowed as the propeller ground to a stop. In a matter of seconds, **I had become a glider.**

My attention switched from inside the cabin to outside. Oil was flowing up the top of the cowling and spread as it hit the windscreen, making forward visibility a problem. Even though I had the highway made, which eased the anxiety slightly, I needed to find a spot without power lines and road signs. With 500 feet of elevation, I stared down looking for just the right spot.

This was going to be a dead-stick landing — no engine. **A little extra airspeed would help in the flare.** One problem I couldn't control was traffic. Automobiles were spread out about every quarter mile.

During emergency training, pilots practice dead-stick landings with the engine idle and prop turning. Now, **the stopped propeller acted like an air brake**, and the plane settled faster than expected. At 300 feet I turned the plane in line with the highway.

With a growing sense of dread I realized the rate of descent made the touchdown spot on a curve in the highway. As I reach for flaps, I spotted a clearing next to the road. A second glance confirmed it: a makeshift runway perfect for a dead engine landing, and the best thing of all — no traffic.

I held my airspeed at 70 knots and turned for the little clearing. By this time the oil completely covered the window, blocking forward visibility. I leaned left and looked around the oil. All visibility would disappear in a few seconds.

Brown smoke trailed the plane, and oil leaked on the exhaust. It was time to get the failing plane on the ground. With the forward visibility nearly gone, **I slipped the plane to see the touchdown area.** With one hundred feet to go, I stared at my chosen landing location.

At first glance it looked like smooth fresh dirt, but now a closer look revealed tree stumps lining the full length of the runway! I glanced back at the highway, but it was too late. I had traded the paved highway for a stump-filled patch of dirt. A feeling of despair and stupidity overwhelmed me. The chance of surviving without a crash approached zero. But I couldn't focus on my bad decision. I had a plane to land. **Maintaining control was absolutely mandatory.**

As the wheels touched dirt, I pushed the nose of the Cessna 185 over enough to see forward and jammed on the left and right brakes to swerve through the obstacle course. **I grimaced as the stumps rolled by the wheels and under the plane.** Some looked high enough to hit the prop. I fought the brakes as the plane skidded back and forth. The tail swung up at an alarming angle. The heavy braking forced the center of gravity forward. Too much pressure would cause the plane to flop on its back.

I fought the controls of the plane until we came to a stop. The elevated tail slammed on the ground with a thud. Miraculously, I had weaved through the stumps.

The adrenalin rush and my shaky hands made exiting the plane difficult. We stared at the tire marks in disbelief. The trail curved through the foot-high tree stumps, missing them by inches.

Closer examination revealed the left front cylinder had blown apart. Two minutes had elapsed from when the problem presented itself to the point of touchdown. An attempted emergency landing while flying the elk survey would have been impossible.

Making the decision to fly the highway saved our lives. From that moment on I made a promise to myself: **fly close to roads or open terrain whenever possible**. This promise has kept me safe and injury-free for years.

We all should learn from the preceding experience. I made a couple of good decisions that day. Following the highway probably saved my passenger's and my life. But I also made a bad decision. I should have landed on the highway. Luckily, this flight ended safely.

My mechanic replaced the broken cylinder, and I flew the plane out of the clearing. I then replaced the engine with a new one. The old engine was contaminated with metal in the oil and I would never have felt comfortable with the repaired engine.

This event made me think a lot about mountain flying and how all pilots need to adhere to the next four rules.

The third *Rule to Live By*: **WHEN POSSIBLE FLY THE SAFEST ROUTE, NOT THE FASTEST.** Arrange your route so that a highway, meadow, or possible landing spots are in close proximity to your flight path.

The fourth *Rule to Live By*: **IN AN EMERGENCY, FLY THE AIRCRAFT AND MAINTAIN CONTROL ALL THE WAY TO THE GROUND.** Having control makes the difference in surviving or not.

The fifth *Rule to Live By*: **NEVER GET INTO A HURRY TO GET ANYWHERE. GET-HOMEITIS KILLS PEOPLE.** Always be ready to turn around to safety.

The sixth *Rule to Live By*: **ONCE YOU CHOOSE A SUR-VIVABLE LANDING SPOT, STICK WITH IT.** If you are absolutely convinced you found a better spot to land, take it. But make sure that if you change locations it's better than the one you're giving up.

The seventh *Rule to Live By*: **IF YOU HAVE A CHOICE, DON'T FLY OVER ROADLESS AREAS IN THE WINTER.** When the engine isn't running smoothly, the road you are flying near becomes your lifeline.

## CHAPTER 2 QUESTIONS:

1. If you have to make an emergency landing while flying over mountainous terrain in the winter, what effect would deep snow have on the landing? _____

   _____

2. What mental effect should a pilot feel when flying near the safety of a road or highway?_____

3. Why should pilots fly the safest routes, not the fastest, while in the mountains? _____

4. When faced with an emergency, why would a pilot turn toward the best emergency landing spot immediately? _____

5. What is the third *Rule to Live By* and explain its meaning. _____

   _____

   _____

6. What is the fourth *Rule to Live By* and explain its meaning. _____

   _____

   _____

7. What is the fifth *Rule to Live By* and explain its meaning. _____

   _____

   _____

8. What is the sixth *Rule to Live By* and explain its meaning. _____

   _____

   _____

9. What is the seventh *Rule to Live By* and explain its meaning. _____

   _____

   _____

# CHAPTER 3:

# MOUNTAIN WIND

**When flying in the mountains wind can be your best friend *or your worst enemy.*** Most of time, wind is your worst enemy. If we could choose between windy or calm in the mountains, almost all pilots would elect the latter. On rare occasions when the air is calm, a pilot can fly closer to the peaks and ridges. We all enjoy seeing an occasional elk or bear standing on a mountain ridge, but this requires flying closer to the ground.

With any kind of wind at all, flying low is next to impossible and sometimes suicidal. **Wind should be the deciding factor to go or stay home when flying in mountains.**

When planning a flight the first thing to get is a good weather briefing. This will give you a basic understanding of winds and the weather system along your route.

**If the forecasted weather is poor conditions and deteriorating, then change your trip plans** until the weather improves. Most of the time the weather briefer will tell you visual flight rules (VFR) is not recommended. But the Flight Service Station will give that answer often when getting weather for mountain flights. Let them know you still want the present weather conditions and the forecasted weather.

If any cold or warm fronts are forecast within a couple of days of your departure time, you can bet **the wind will get stronger and the cloud cover will lower.** If no fronts are predicted, chances are flying in the mountains will be possible.

If wind at the mountaintops is forecasted to be 30 knots or faster, the corresponding wind speed in the draws and canyons could be 50 or 60 knots. Wind speed will increase as it's being pressed between mountains in the passes and at ridge tops. The turbulence created from that much wind could spell big trouble for an unsuspecting pilot. **If wind predictions are high, wait for better conditions.**

Now, I'm not saying you can't fly in mountains when wind is blowing. It's done every day. But downdrafts can lift you off the seat or updrafts can push you down in the seat, making for uncomfortable flying conditions. Neither situation is pleasant; you could be fighting for control of the plane.

There is nothing scarier than not knowing if you will survive a flight or wondering if the plane will stay together. **If you hit turbulence that makes you light in the seat, turn back** out of the rough air and wait for better conditions.

The eighth *Rule to Live By* is: **IF THE FORECASTED WIND AT THE MOUNTAIN TOPS IS 30 KNOTS -- STAY HOME.**

The clouds in the picture to the left are flattened out. What is causing these clouds to have a drawn-out appearance?

At first glance this cloud formation should tell a pilot there are high winds in the area. Probably not a good place to fly, but a second glance should reveal a few more things.

The bottom and top of the clouds are flat and smooth. This means although there are high winds, flying close and directly under or on top of these clouds should give you a fairly smooth ride. This information comes in handy if you don't have any other option but to fly through the area.

Another thing to remember is the weather forecast you get from the Flight Service Station is a forecast. An educated guess at best and most likely it will be different than what you experience. The weather briefer is doing the best he/she can, but due to the complexity of the turbulent flow, the only true test may be to take a look for yourself. Just be ready to turn around if it is something you don't like.

Another consideration is many forecasts are made from weather balloons. The Weather Service tracks the balloon as it rises in the atmosphere and monitors the direction and speed of drift. This is the information relayed to you until another balloon is sent skyward. What you are receiving could be several hours old. **Take the forecast for what it is, a forecast.**

**The only weather you can trust while flying in the mountains is the weather you can see out the windows of your airplane.** So, you must know cloud formations and what those formations represent.

The cloud formation to the above shows what happens as the wind speeds up while flowing over mountain ranges. These lenticular clouds are drawn out for 20 miles, and are up around 20,000 feet. The jet stream has dipped and created wind conditions a small airplane might not handle well. The wind at ground level was blowing 30 knots while this high formation grew in layers. With that much wind on the ground, and stronger winds at higher altitude, I would sit on the ground and wait for another day to fly.

The picture to the left shows the same high lenticular clouds, but this shows the downwind side of the cloud. The cloud is dipping toward the ground. As it descends and speeds up, the wind tumbles and rolls. The cloud is breaking apart, creating dangerous up and downdrafts. Even though the cloud is disappearing, the invisible wind is still present. More than one unsuspecting pilot has flown into these turbulent conditions only to experience a rough, unpleasant ride. You can bet they won't fly around this type of cloud formation again.

How can a pilot tell how fast the wind is blowing before he leaves the ground? A wise plan is to stop at an airstrip close to your route and ask local pilots. Also, get in the habit of looking at cloud formations. In time, you will be able to get an idea of wind speed and direction on the ground.

The best way to determine windspeed while still on the ground is to use the tail of the plane or any vertical object and look past the object at the clouds in the distance. **Hold your head still, and look through your vertical object to the clouds.** Try to use clouds at about a 45% angle up from the ground and ten miles or further away. **If you can see movement in the clouds from that distance, the wind is blowing strong at the cloud altitude.**

While flying, a pilot can read wind speed and direction by looking at cloud shadows on the ground. The speed of the shadow moving across the ground is the same speed and direction as the wind at cloud

altitude. It can be hard to judge the speed of the shadow, but if its movement is easily recognizable, the clouds making the shadow are moving fairly fast.

The clouds in the picture to the left formed over the ridge just north of Shafer Meadows in Montana's Bob Marshall Wilderness. Shafer can be a rough, bumpy place to fly during the heat of the day when the wind is blowing. On this day we were hauling rafting people in and out of the Meadows and had just landed as the odd-shaped clouds grew in intensity to the east of our location. Wind on the ground was 25 knots out of the west, and the wind at the cloud layer, 9000 feet up, was about 30 knots. The edges of the clouds were rough, sharp-pointed, and uneven. On the departure, **we encountered turbulent up and downdrafts, and at times the plane would shutter almost out of control.** The wind seemed to be blowing in no definite direction. The only thing to do was to **slow the plane below maneuvering speed**, tighten the seat belts, and hang on. We had to make the flight, but if I were flying for pleasure I wouldn't have been there. The ride was just too uncomfortable.

**Usually your best bet to get out of a rough and bumpy wind is to climb higher.** Lenticular clouds indicate high winds at altitude, but if the top of the lens-shaped cloud is smooth and flat, it is possible to fly just above the cloud. The ride is usually smooth, and if you're going the right direction it's possible to get a big gain in ground speed. But if you're flying into the wind, it would be wiser to find a lower route below the high-speed wind.

I have tried to fly over lenticular clouds that capped the mountains. After climbing my Super Cub for 30 minutes to get above the clouds, I found how strong the winds really were. When I leveled the plane, the ground speed was near zero. I dropped back down to near ground level to avoid the winds and flew back to my home base to wait for a better day.

If you are ever flying close to the top of a lenticular cloud, there is one thing you must do: get away from the cloud before it starts its downward movement. You don't want to be anywhere close to the turbulence created from the wind that is breaking apart. Just because the cloud disappears doesn't mean the wind diminishes. The high winds roll and descend as the air spreads downward. Your wisest bet is to stay clear of lenticular clouds and plan your flight path so your route won't pass through the downwind side of these clouds.

The cloud formation on the next page formed over Glacier National Park. The upper group of clouds indicates very high-speed winds and rough air. The curve in the cloud shows that not very far to the right, the wind is descending at a high rate of speed. A cloud formation has developed on the downwind side of every peak. The wind is rolling and descending. This type of turbulent wind can knock a light plane out of the sky or bend the control surfaces. Any flying below the high clouds and downwind of the high mountain peak would probably be impossible. A glimpse of nature's awesome strength is beautiful when you're a distance away, but should demand a 180-degree turn to safety while flying.

Clouds form when moisture-laden air rises. When the air is saturated and the temperature right, a cloud is formed. **When clouds form, air movement or wind is present. A pilot has to learn how to read this air movement and then fly where the wind will create the smoothest ride.**

While flying, if you can't figure out by looking at the clouds or you don't have any visual clues on the ground about the wind, trim the plane for level flight. If there is wind, the plane should drift downwind or across the ground at an angle. The way you drift is the way the wind is blowing.

Another way to tell is to trim the plane for level flight and let the plane fly, hands-off. **The tail of the plane will blow downwind.** So, if the tail of the plane isn't directly behind, but to the right a little bit, the wind is blowing from your left. A mountain pilot needs to know how he can use this knowledge to help him get through the mountains.

Wind blowing on a high mountain lake can also give a pilot im

portant information. The picture above shows smooth water along the right shoreline, and wind hitting the lake in about the middle and to the left shoreline. This indicates air flows over the peaks to the right of the lake, then continues down to the water in the middle of the lake and to the left.

This should tell a pilot that flying close to the peaks and over the top of the lake will produce a left crosswind with down turbulent air. A plane might handle the turbulence from the wind rolling over the ridge, but an unsuspecting pilot won't soon forget the sinking air as the plane descends toward the lake.

Rule Number 5, never get into a hurry to get anywhere, would come into effect here: take the time to circle higher before crossing over the lake and ridge. In this case there is plenty of cloud clearance to climb before flying into the disturbed air. **A pilot always has to have the state of mind to never get in a hurry or he/she will end up in trouble.**

Our goal as pilots is to interpret the clues the clouds give us about wind conditions. In time you'll be able to look at clouds and understand what type of wind or weather created the formation.

On the next page is the Chinese Wall, located in the Bob Marshall Wilderness. The wall has a 2000-foot vertical cliff that runs 15 miles. The puffy clouds above the wall show wind flowing over the

peaks and then moving downwind. The bottom of the cloud is smooth indicating it would be a smooth ride below the clouds.

Usually the weather around the wall is windy and turbulent. Above the puffy cloud is clear blue sky, no lenticular clouds in the area.

This would be the best ride.

The picture to the left also indicates a perfect day to fly. No clouds, which in turn means not much wind. Snow blowing off the peaks would also indicate wind, but none is present. This picture shows a glacier in Glacier National Park. Viewing sights like this is one reason I became a pilot. But keep your distance from the downwind side of these peaks. In addition to keeping your distance, **always leave an escape route** so you can turn away from the rocks and enjoy the sights.

The wind direction in high altitudes will probably differ from wind down in the mountains, especially earlier in the day. If winds aloft are out of west then the winds near ground level will usually blow up and down the deep canyons, even if the canyons run north to south. As **the sun rises the increasing temperature will cause lower winds to increase in speed and mix with higher altitude wind at the mountain tops.** Where the air mixes is the bumpiest ride, especially on the downwind side of the ridges.

As the temperature continues to rise, the high winds at altitude descend further into the mountain canyons creating gusty and turbulent flying conditions. **During the hottest time of day, the mixing air will be the roughest all the way to the valley floors.** Added air rolling off the back side of ridges can make flying impossible. As the sun descends in the afternoon and evening approaches the same process with the air plays out, but in reverse. Right before dark the air smooths out.

If you want a smooth ride fly early in the morning and stay late. I'm not a fan of flying mid to late afternoon in the mountains. Which bring us to the next rule.

The ninth *Rule to Live By*: **FLY EARLY IN THE MORNING OR LATE IN THE EVENING.** Arrange your flight time so you are not flying in the heat of the day. The smoothest air is usually in the morning or late evening.

The tenth *Rule to Live By*: **Up-air IS GOOD, down-air IS BAD.** A mountain pilot should always try to find air that is rising as it's usually smoother and lessens the work load on the plane. Plan your route of flight to stay away from downdrafts that create turbulence. Turbulence does more than just make you and your passengers uncomfortable. It adds stress on the aircraft which in time weakens the airframe.

CHAPTER 3 QUESTIONS:

1. When flying in the mountains, why can wind be your best friend or your worst enemy? _____

2. What should be the first thing a pilot should do when planning a trip into the mountains? _____

3. If a cold or warm front is forecasted, what will the winds be doing? _____

4. What flight conditions can be expected if the wind is getting stronger? _____

5. If winds at the mountain tops are high, what will the winds in the canyons, draws, and passes be doing? _____

6. What is the eighth *Rule to Live By*? _____

7. Why is it hard to get a good mountain weather forecast? _____

8. What weather can a mountain pilot trust? _____

9. How can a pilot tell the wind speed and direction while still on the ground? _____

10. How can a pilot read what the wind is doing while flying? _____

11. What is usually the best plan of action to get out of bumpy wind? _____

12. What will the tail of your aircraft do when flying in level flight? _____

13. How can the wind on a high mountain lake help a pilot tell what the winds are doing? _____

14. A mountain pilot should always have what state of mind? _____

15. When fly close to the downwind side of a lenticular cloud, what does a pilot need to do? _____

16. When flying close to steep vertical cliffs, a pilot should do what?

_____

17. Explain why a mountain pilot should fly early and stay late.

_____

18. What is the ninth *Rule to Live By*? _____

19. What is the tenth *Rule to Live By* and explain its purpose. _____

_____

_____

# CHAPTER 4:

# KNOWING WHERE TO FLY

Mountain pilots are always hunting for smooth air and the best ride. The question to be answered is, **how does a mountain pilot know where to fly and how can he pick the best route to get there?** One way already briefly discussed is to hunt for rising air. To accomplish this we need to figure out where the wind is coming from and how the plane will react to the flow as we fly around ridges, canyons, peaks, and long narrow valleys. With this knowledge the pilot will fly from ridge to ridge, or updraft to updraft, as they move through the mountains. At times the plane will fly out of the updraft, but the prepared pilot won't panic, because he has already figured out where the next updraft is and has planned his route accordingly.

Pilots need to visualize the flow of air as it moves through the mountains. **One of the best ways to learn about air patterns is to watch water flow down a creek.** The water is reacting to the rocks the same way as air in the mountains reacts to the mountain rocks.

As the water flows, it changes speed and direction as it travels beside and between the rocks. The water surges up and over big boulders and then drops in behind and below the rock. The water doesn't flow out smoothly but instead stays behind the rock, churning. Eventually it flows out from behind the rock and continues downstream in a smooth flow until it is interrupted by another rock.

As the water moves between two rocks the pressure speeds the water up, and then the water tumbles turbulently behind the rock. The flow of water pushed off the rocks collides with more water, creating white water or turbulent flow. When the water slowly moves away from the rocks and flattens out, it flows smoothly. Analyze the water flow over a 2-foot drop to a flat rock below. As it goes over the drop the water

churns, speeds up, and when it hits the bottom, spreads out and flies in different directions from the force of the water slamming on top.

As you visualize the water flowing and churning ask yourself, **"Where would be the best place to float if I were in a canoe?"** Obviously not where the white water is, but you would paddle around the turbulence.

You can see now how visualizing the flow of water is similar to a pilot thinking about airflow through the mountains. The air flows up and over ridges and tumbles down the back side of a ridge, speeding up as it is squeezed between mountain ridges. Air slows along flat ground creating a smooth flow until it reacts to ground friction and increases in speed as it starts up the next mountain peak or ridge. The smooth flow or rising air is where a mountain pilot would want to fly. The "white water", or turbulent air is where a pilot avoids. The faster the flow of air, the faster the wind

climbs, drops, and flows around the mountains. **Turbulence increases and decreases with wind speed.**

Hopefully this visualization exercise gives you a mental picture of your surroundings in the mountains. As you fly over ridges, peaks and valleys you will experience turbulence as the wind speed increases, decreases, and changes direction. Remember the flow of water in the creek and visualize the air flowing through the mountains.

**Don't get caught sleeping and be blown over the top of a ridge into down-air on the back side.** A rotor or rolling air hangs near the top of the ridge on the downwind side. If you get pushed over, your smooth ride will turn unpleasant fast and could bring an end to a good day. If that does happen, the plane will try to roll in the direction the wind is rolling. Try to stop the roll with control inputs. Keep up your speed and add all available power to stop the downward rolling motion.

Then fly directly away from the ridge creating the down-air. Remember that the turbulent air will flatten as it flows away from the ridge. It will flow uphill when it hits the next ridge. This climbing air is what a mountain pilot wants.

If while flying along a ridge with up-air and the updraft subsides or the ridge ends, it would be wise to make a 180-degree turn and fly along the same ridge you had just flown along instead of flying out of the updraft. The pilot just used the up-air, and he knows where to find the updraft. Why not use the same updraft one more time and use it to climb above the turbulence.

The figure on the opposite page shows a typical mountain pattern in the Rocky Mountains. It also shows the flow of air, turbulence, smooth air, updrafts, and downdrafts. By now, you should be able to visualize the smoothest routes to fly through this mountain range.

Line A has smooth air with a tailwind. Altitude gets a pilot above the friction created by the mountains and would be the best place to fly if cloud cover permits.

Line B would also have smooth air.

Line C would have an updraft flow with smooth air.

Line D would have a downdraft flow and turbulent air, not a place to fly for any length of time. Even though a pilot could fly through this area, the flight path should be planned so the time spent in this area is minimized and the next updraft is close.

Line E has turbulent air with downdrafts -- not a place to fly. Depending on the wind speed, an underpowered airplane would struggle to fly out of the down flow. Although, if a pilot can fly through Area E, the wind will climb up the next ridge. By making a right turn and following the updraft ridge the ride should be smooth. The ridge is long enough to give the pilot time to climb above the turbulent air before leaving the ridge.

Line F shows wind being squeezed between ridges. It is speeding up and the air could be turbulent -- not a place to fly.

Line G shows air being pressured between two ridges. As the pilot nears the back of the draw, he will have to climb up and over the ridge or turn around and fly back down. Trying to climb uphill while flying low in a mountain valley can turn into a disaster. The steep walls of the canyon might outclimb the performance of the airplane. **Never fly uphill while flying low in mountain valleys or draws; it is possible to stall an airplane if you pull the nose of the airplane up while trying to climb over the ridge or turn around. If you are going to fly low in a high mountain draw or valley, always fly downhill.**

Line H shows up-air flowing up a ridge. Just remember, what goes up will eventually come down. Have your flight path prepared so that you don't get caught in the turbulent air at area E.

Line I –This area is called the demarcation line and would have a smooth flow of air right on top of the ridge. Air just a few feet over the ridge will be turbulent. This area is usually only used by helicopters. Flying close to the ridge top would be dangerous for a airplane pilot. If you fly in this area, use extreme caution.

Let's review the possibilities: Line A, at the top, would be the best and smoothest ride because cloud cover isn't there to stop your climb to an altitude above turbulence created by mountain friction. Line B shows the smooth airflow across the wide valley. As wind hits the mountain it starts to climb up and over. This updraft is the lifting action mountain pilots covet. As you can see from the figure, you will have a smooth ride all way to Position I, and then the wind descends down the backside of the ridge, indicated by Position D. At this spot you will encounter a downdraft with turbulence, a problem for pilots.

The severity of the turbulence is related to the wind speed. The more wind, the rougher it gets. It is possible to get sucked down behind a ridge and not be able to climb back up to safety.

As turbulent air flows down toward the bottom of the canyons, it eventually hits the next ridge and starts to flow up the next ridge. The air moving up is smooth and helps the plane in the climb. You can see in the figure there is turbulent air on the downwind side and behind all the peaks, ridges, and cliffs. A pilot has to be able to visualize where this turbulent air is before he or she crosses over mountains. Always pick the safest and smoothest route.

If I couldn't fly high enough to get above the turbulence, I would fly the following route: fly Line B at the top of the figure, use the updraft at Position C, then fly directly away from the ridge at Position I, trying not to descend. Use all available power, keep the wings level and fly the plane at maneuvering speed. I don't want to descend below the ridges.

What is maneuvering speed? Maneuvering speed **is the speed at which full deflection of the controls will not result in any damage to the aircraft, or safe speed.** Know the maneuvering speed of your aircraft and fly at that speed when hitting turbulence.

Above Position E, there is a line that says, "Up-air, calm ride." When in this position—and coming off of Line D—I would make a right turn and follow the smooth air flowing up the ridge. Stay along the ridge for as long as the smooth up-air exists.

When the ridge ends, the good ride will end. At this point, I would already be looking for more up-air on the next ridge or make a 180-degree turn to fly back along the same ridge I had just followed, which would cause the aircraft to climb. As I climbed up, I would look for the next up-air ridge and then continue through the mountains using this technique.

**Crossing mountain ranges in windy conditions is a process of flying from updraft to updraft.** Remember water flow in a creek, and take time to study it. Clear water is smooth water or in this case air, and white water represents turbulence in the air.

Apply the water model to airflow in the picture on the next page. Which way is the wind blowing? Where is the smooth up-air, and where will it end and turn into down-air and turbulence? By using this mountain flying technique you should have a better understanding of where to fly and where not to fly.

Remember wind speed increases along ridge tops, canyons, and mountain peaks, so if the wind is strong at altitude, down in the mountains the wind speed and turbulence could triple. If you encounter an extreme downdraft and full power doesn't stop the rate of descent, it is time to take action. Don't sit and wait for something to happen! Hitting the ground might be what happens.

Figure out a way to fly out of the downdraft before it's too late. Maybe a shallow left or right turn, but most of the time flying directly away from the ridge or peak that caused the downdraft will get you out of the downdraft. **Get as far away from it as fast as you can.** Then hunt for up-air to climb back to altitude.

While flying a grizzly bear biologist in Glacier National Park, I flew into a severe downdraft that full power did not abate. The nose of the Super Cub was pointed skyward and the airspeed was 50 mph. **It didn't matter what I did, I could not stop the rate of descent.**

With the ground rushing up at the floundering plane, I had only one option left. I shoved the nose of the plane over into a near vertical angle. We stared straight out the front windscreen at the spot where we would hit the ground. The airspeed climbed to a red line. The excessive speed forced wind over the airplane control surfaces, and gave me control over the severe downdraft. I gently leveled the plane as the steep mountainside leveled at the bottom of the canyon. We continued down-stream at 100 feet above the canyon bottom and just below the wind to safety.

**If I had waited we would have slammed into the bottom of the canyon.** The extra energy created from the excessive airspeed gave me control over the extreme downdraft. This energy made it possible to dive down and away from the life threatening wind The maneuver was extreme, and not one I would recommend to another pilot. But it saved our lives.

I had tested the air before I entered the canyon, but still flew into the extreme downdraft. If you have ever heard that downdrafts never hit the ground--**don't believe it.** I flew over the area a few days later in the same spot where I dove toward the ground and saw the results of that powerful downdraft. **All of the trees were smashed down and lying on the ground in a circular arrangement.** That wind not only hit the ground, but it crushed the trees in its path. I'm sorry to say my passenger never flew in an airplane again, but he's alive to talk about it.

## CHAPTER 4 QUESTIONS:

1. While flying in the mountains, a pilot should hunt for _____ _____air.

2. A mountain pilot will fly from ridge to ridge, hunting for up-air. What information does he need to know to accomplish this?

   _____

   _____

3. What can a pilot use to visualize the air flow around mountains?

   _____

4. What increases or decreases with wind speed? _____

   _____

5. Why would a mountain pilot want to fly near the top of a ridge and on the upwind side? _____

   _____

6. What would a pilot do if he gets caught in down turbulent air on the backside of a ridge? _____

   _____

7. Why would a pilot never fly up a high mountain valley or draw?

   _____

   _____

8. What is maneuvering speed and what does that speed guarantee?

   _____

   _____

9. Flying through the mountains in windy conditions is a process of flying from_____ to _____.

10. Does extreme downdraft air ever hit the ground? _____

    _____

# CHAPTER 5:

# DEATH IN GLACIER NATIONAL PARK

The pilot of a Piper PA-20 left the Plains, Montana airport on a flight plan to Lethbridge, Alberta. A weather system had stalled over western Montana with bases of clouds at about 6000 feet. The mountaintops were obscured with small openings between the ridges and the cloud base. If the pilot flew a straight line to his destination, he would cross over some of the steepest and most dangerous mountains in the United States.

**The pilot had the option of crossing over the rugged mountains or flying a safer route.** By following Highway 2, the pilot could fly around the south end of the dangerous mountains and have the added **benefit of a highway to follow.**

After half an hour of flight the pilot came to the spot where he would need to make a decision: fly straight forward and hope to find an opening between the rocky ridges and the cloud base, or fly the highway. The highway route would take about 30 minutes longer. The pilot made the wrong choice; he elected to fly into the peaks of Glacier National Park.

It wasn't a good day to fly in the mountains. I had canceled my wolf survey flight on that same day because of the high winds. It would have been too turbulent for my Cessna 185, and it would have been suicidal in a PA-20. Then you add low clouds with rain and snow showers, and the flight across the Park was doomed before it even got started.

A pilot that was hiking in the area saw the yellow Piper flying toward the dangerous peaks of the park. She could hear the engine change sounds as the pilot fought to maintain control of the small plane. In seconds he was out of sight. A minute later she heard the sound of the plane and felt relieved as the plane reversed its course and headed back the way he came.

She was shocked to see the plane reverse its course again and head back into the dangerous mountains. The snow was blowing off all the ridges with estimated winds to 60 mph. As the pilot fought to maintain control, the ground observer feared there was no way he would survive.

**Mountains take on a new appearance when clouds are hanging below the peaks and ridges.** The wind speed and therefore turbulence increases as the air gets squeezed between peaks. In the low cloud cover the pilot would have to find an opening between the ridge and the base of the clouds. As he flew across the continental divide, the plane was forced dangerously close to the top of the ridge.

**The downdraft and turbulence off the back side of the sharp mountain ridge could tear a small plane apart.** That is exactly what happened.

The wreckage of the yellow plane was found two days later. The pilot had flown through the small opening and then slammed into the ground at a tremendous speed. The engine rolled down the hill a couple thousand feet further and ended up in a small lake below. The pilot died on impact.

If he would have followed the highway, he would have had a rough flight, but one that was survivable. He broke four of the *Rules to Live By*, and it cost him his life.

Rule 1 - Be prepared. The pilot wasn't prepared to make the right decision to fly or not fly.

Rule 2 - If caution isn't used, people can get hurt. If a pilot flies in the mountains, he will fly into bad weather. That's a given. He must be able to make the decision to fly out of the bad weather to safer conditions before it's too late.

Rule 3 - Fly the safest route, not the fastest. The pilot had a safer route that would have made the flight feasible.

Rule 4 - If you have a choice, do not fly over roadless areas in the winter. The pilot had the chance to use the safety of a highway all the way to his destination, but chose against it and paid the ultimate price.

## CHAPTER 5 QUESTIONS:

1.  Why should a mountain pilot fly the safest route?

    _____

    _____

2.  What can the strong downdrafts and turbulence do to a small air-
    craft? _____

    _____

3.  What four *Rules to Live By* did the pilot break and explain each.

    _____

    _____

    _____

    _____

# CHAPTER 6:

# WEATHER MAKER

Flying in the mountains when the weather has obscured the top of the mountain can test any mountain pilot. Your route of flight might be blue skies and endless visibility until you enter the mountains.

Excitement from finally entering the mountains might be short-lived when the visibility drops to a mile and the cloud cover seems to be lowering. It's time to fly back to the good weather. After you land at an airport just out of the mountains, you'll sit down and look at the cloud-covered ridges in the distance wondering why the weather you just encountered wasn't mentioned in your preflight briefing.

**Mountains make their own weather.** The sky around a big mountain range might be clear blue, but in the mountains it's completely different. A pilot has to be able to interpret what the weather is doing and be able to act accordingly.

**The weather you are looking at out the window of the plane is the weather you must read and understand,** not the weather depicted on a weather chart.

If you are flying up a canyon with cloud cover that obscures the mountaintop, **you should fly as high as possible and close to the base of the clouds.** This flying position will give you the maximum mountain clearance and room to turn around. Be careful not to fly accidentally into the bottom of the cloud base. If the clouds lower, you must lower your elevation to stay out of the clouds.

The last place to fly is down low in mountain canyons. Canyons get narrower as you lower your elevation. It is possible to fly so low in a canyon that you won't have enough room to make a 180 degree turn in case of an emergency.

**Remember the wind will be under more pressure down low in canyons, which in turn makes more turbulence and downdrafts.**

The safest place to position your airplane while flying along mountain valleys is on the upwind side and near the top of the ridge. Fly as high as possible and close to the base of the clouds.

Flying in the mountains with only a mile of visibility is simply asking for disaster. Unless you know your route like the back of your hand, turn back to safety immediately.

Set your limits and when that limit is reached, retreat before the visibility gets so bad you can't make the turn. Somehow you flew into this bad situation--don't make it worse by waiting to see if the visibility improves!

If you decide to wait, as you can see from the picture at the left, the weather visibility could get to the point where you can't make the turn safely. **As the visibility deteriorates, it gets harder to judge how far a mountain is from the plane.** This is where your instrument training will finally pay off. If you are having trouble seeing the ridge you passed a few seconds earlier you are getting deeper into no-man's land. In seconds the visibility will drop to near zero as shown on the next picture. **You're in trouble,** but fight off the panic -- start the U-turn that will get you back to safety.

Remember, the slower the speed the faster the rate of turn. By slowing the plane you will be able to turn in a smaller area. The tendency is to pull the nose up as the outline of the mountain fades along with the visibility. You could easily stall the plane, so **keep the plane level as you turn.** Add power and flaps to make a steeper turn.

Keep a close eye on the artificial horizon and your airspeed. If you have passengers, have them looking outside to help warn you of danger. After you finally complete the turn and head back to better weather it is time to wipe the sweat from you brow and scold yourself for getting into this situation. You have just broken **the eleventh *Rule to Live By*: WHEN ENTERING LOW FORWARD VISIBILITY, MAKE A 180-DEGREE TURN IMMEDIATELY**. Waiting to see if the visibility improves could get you killed.

If you fly a lot in the mountains, you will eventually find yourself in the situation described above. Weather in the mountains can change in a matter of minutes. Light rain in the evenings will put a lot of moisture on the ground. The next morning will dawn with the whole mountain range fogged in.

If you choose to camp at a wilderness airstrip, you could be stuck there for days. Most of the time around 11:00 a.m. the fog will start to dissipate and be gone by early afternoon. Do not wait around too long. The fog might return around 5:00 in the evening.

When flying past a fogged-over wilderness airstrip, sometimes you can look straight down and see the runway. The picture on the next page has a mountain airstrip roughly in the middle of the photo. The unsuspecting pilot might assume the fog is thin enough for him to make

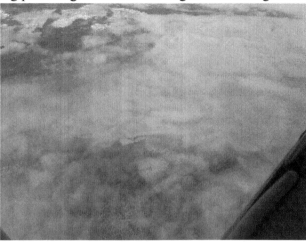

a landing approach.

But be aware that once you fly into the fog, you will lose all forward visibility and outside reference. You'll be flying in the dark. Not a pleasant thought. Never enter any fog formation while flying in the mountains.

Sometimes you'll be flying in clear rough air at altitude with fog hanging low in the valleys. If increasing your altitude doesn't make for a better ride, try flying just above the fog. If fog is present and not moving, then you can assume there is no wind to create turbulence near the fog. You will find your smooth ride right above the fog, but be careful not to fly into the fog.

The twelfth *Rule to Live By*: **NEVER FLY INTO FOG OR CLOUDS WHILE IN THE MOUNTAINS.**

The question remains, how do we fly through the mountains when the weather isn't perfect? If you wait for clear blue skies and unlimited visibility you may end up never flying in the mountains. **Knowing the area around your flight path is important.**

It is good to know what is around the next bend or where the river valley takes a sharp right turn. But you may not always be familiar with your route, so here are some general guidelines.

**Flying up a river drainage is always better than trying to cross over ridgelines** to find your airstrip. If the weather shrouds the mountain tops it would make it a lot easier if you can fly around the ridges and into the same drainage as your landing spot. **While flying in the drainage, it is imperative that a pilot must be able to see the ground all the time and always be able to see the next finger ridge ahead.**

Remember, fly up one side of the canyon, and leave plenty of room to turn around. As you fly around a bend of the drainage, if you can't see any landmarks ahead, it is time to turn around. Turn back before it is too late. By slowing the airplane, you will have more time to see what is coming up. Keep looking upstream as you turn. Sometimes the clouds will be lying against the side of the canyons but not in the middle of the drainage.

Remember though, if the middle of the drainage is clear of clouds and you have to fly in the middle of the draw, you will not have the same amount of area to use if you must turn around. The picture on the previous page shows why you never fly in the fog or clouds. There's Rockies in them there clouds.

As you fly up the canyon toward your destination, the drainage will usually narrow. This could cause the cloud cover to descend, and in turn force a pilot to lower his elevation to stay out of the clouds. Don't get caught daydreaming and end up in a trap you can't get out of. Avoid flying too low without enough room to turn around. Always leave yourself an out, or a place to get out of trouble.

**The thirteenth *Rule to Live By*: ALWAYS FLY UP ONE SIDE OF A CANYON, AND LEAVE PLENTY OF ROOM TO TURN AROUND.**

In most airplanes the pilot sits on the left side of the cabin. His best view is forward and to the right. If you must turn around, try to plan a turn to the right so a door post or the wing doesn't obstruct your view. **In the turn the pilot can lean forward and look past the front of the wing and see any objects** that could present a problem. The next picture shows the canyon narrowing down with lowering clouds. Extreme caution needs to be used since room to turn around is running out real quick.

The next question to be answered is, do I turn into a downdraft or an updraft? If you're flying on the preferred side of the canyon, you should be flying on the updraft side.

As you turn the plane around it is possible to fly out of the up-air and fly into the down-air that is flowing over the ridge on the opposite side of the canyon. This is the reason to slow the plane, and **turn back as quickly and safely as possible.** Fly back over the same route you flew up by retracing your flight path, only in the opposite direction. Now is when a moving GPS map comes in handy. A dotted line on the screen indicates your flight path, making it easy to follow it out of the mountains.

Remember you are flying in a machine. Machines do have mechanical problems. But, if your airplane is maintained well, chances of having mechanical problems are slim.

Mountain pilots need to know how to put the odds of surviving on their sides. **One way to do this is fly the safest routes, stay as high as possible, and always leave an escape route.**

The picture to the left shows clouds flowing over the top of a ridge and moving downward. Flying close to the top and left side of the ridge would put you in downdrafts and turbulent air. **A pilot wants to maintain his distance from the air flowing over a ridge.** The clear sky above the clouds leaves plenty of room to fly high enough to stay out of the down-air on the left side.

The center picture shows wind blowing snow up a high mountain ridge. The airplane is flying along with almost no power, and it is

soaring along the ridge just like an eagle. The air is rising, creating a smooth updraft. A dream flight.

The next picture shows clouds rolling over a ridge and down the side of a mountain. Air between the clouds and the airplane will be turbulent and gain in intensity as you near the mountain.

**As you are approaching a mountain shrouded in clouds, climb before you get to the rough air or to a downdraft.** If a weather system is in the area and a solid cloud layer obscures the ridges, a climb

might be impossible. At this point you need to look for an opening between the ridge and the base of the clouds. Remember the wind is stronger and more turbulent right along the top of the ridge or on the downwind side of the ridge. Anywhere the wind is being pressured between mountains and ridges, turbulence is probable.

Be prepared to make a 180-degree turn at the first sign of rolling or down-air. If you're not sure about the degree of turbulence you might fly into or how much your plane can handle, keep your speed up and make a high-speed pass by the area in question. Speed is energy, and excess energy can get you out of trouble.

Approach the ridge at a 45-degree angle, rather than straight on, making a turn back to clean air easier. When you get close to crossing over the ridge or turning up the next draw, you should be able to see through to the area on the other side.

**Never cross a ridge or mountain unless you are positive the weather on the other side is flyable.** Always leave room to make a turn away from the opening. Be absolutely sure it is safe to continue.

The picture to the right shows a narrow mountain canyon with clouds obscuring the upper sides of the ridges. The rain droplets on the windscreen are cutting your visibility. Remember that mountains make their own weather. It can rain so hard in the mountains you can lose all forward visibility.

If that happens, most of the time a pilot will be able to look straight down and remain in visual contact of the ground. But, if you don't know the area, you are basically flying blind. When forward visibility drops to less than a mile, it is time to retreat to safety!

**By flying close to the ridge on the upwind side of a canyon, you will have room and be prepared to turn around.**

The picture on the next page shows a small clearance between the ridge and the base of the clouds. The clouds flowing off the backside of the peak in the center of the photo show the wind blowing from the left to the right.

That should tell you anywhere to the right of ridge will be downdraft and turbulent air. Be ready to turn away from the ridge at the first sign of a downdraft. If the wind is strong enough, it might be wise to find a better spot that has more room to maneuver the plane and cross over the ridge.

Freezing rain is a scary forecast for mountain pilots. Anytime you are in visible moisture you run the risk of getting ice on the plane. The temperature where you are flying might be 10 degrees, which is well below freezing. You wouldn't think there would be a possibility of freezing rain at that temperature, but if a warm front has moved into the area and trapped the cold air below, any rain passing down through the cold air will turn to ice the second it hits the surface of the plane.

Freezing rain will hit on the windscreen of your airplane. As it accumulates, your visibility will start to diminish. Don't wait to see if it stops. Fly back into clear air. Ice can add up so quickly the plane could accumulate enough to stop the lifting action of the wings. **Freezing rain is one of the most dangerous weather phenomena** that a pilot can get into.

**The fourteenth *Rule to Live By*: NEVER FLY IN FREEZING RAIN.**

## CHAPTER 6 QUESTIONS:

1.  What weather does a mountain pilot have to know how to interpret?
    _____

2.  When flying upstream in a draw, a pilot should fly where? _____
    _____

3.  Why does a mountain pilot not fly low in the bottom of a canyon?
    _____

4.  When the visibility drops to a mile or less, what must you do?
    _____

5.  As visibility deteriorates, it gets harder and harder to do what?
    _____

6.  What happens to rate of turn as the plane's airspeed lowers?
    _____

7.  What is the eleventh *Rule to Live By*? _____
    _____

8.  Rain in the evening usually means what will be present the next morning? _____

9.  What happens to forward visibility when flying in fog? _____
    _____

10. What is the twelfth *Rule to Live By*? _____
    _____

11. Why is knowing the area you're flying in important? _____
    _____

12. Why does a mountain pilot fly up the side of the canyon? _____
    _____

13. What is the thirteenth *Rule to Live By*? _____
    _____

14. When making a 180 degree turn, does the pilot turn into the updraft or downdraft? _____

15. What does a mountain pilot need to do to put the odds of surviving an emergency on his side? _____
    _____

16. When wind is being pressured between mountains, what is probable? _____
    _____

17. What is airspeed? Airspace? _____

_____

18. Rain in the mountains can create what? _____

19. When forward visibility drops to less than a mile, what should a mountain pilot do? _____

20. If a mountain pilot encounters freezing rain, what would be his best plan of action? _____

21. What is the fourteenth *Rule to Live By*? _____

_____

# CHAPTER 7:

# LANDINGS & TAKEOFFS FROM HIGH MOUNTAIN AIRSTRIPS

After flying around mountains peaks and ridges you have finally found your destination runway. It's hidden down in the bottom of a high mountain valley, and doesn't look long enough. Rest assured it's long enough. But now you need to think of the best way to get down to and land on the grass airstrip safely.

If a strong wind is blowing at altitude, the wise thing to do is **keep your altitude and fly over the airstrip.** Usually windsocks will be on either end or the middle of the runway.

Before you can decide the best route to fly to get down to the runway you need to know what the wind is doing. The wind at a higher altitude will not be the same as the wind at the airstrip. Canyons and deep draws filter the air and change its direction to flow with the direction of the canyons.

As we learned earlier, **as wind is pressured between ridges,**

**draws and canyons, wind speed and turbulence increase.** It is possible to fly through wind blowing in many directions and at different speeds. As you do, expect the plane to react to the different winds as it flies through them. **One second you'll be flying straight and level, then sideways, and the next second you'll be slammed down. Expect the unexpected.**

If you find yourself in a downdraft over a runway, adjust your power to stop the rate of descent. If power doesn't stop the descent then change your direction so that you fly out of the downdraft. This could mean making a right downwind or an abnormal approach.

Standard approaches might not be possible while landing at a mountain airstrip. It all depends on the direction and strength of the wind. Be ready to change the approach to fit the situation. **The only things that a pilot can count on while flying in the mountains are turbulence, wind direction changes, and high density altitude.**

It would be a wise practice to fly as close to your airstrip as possible in case of emergencies, but don't fly close to or behind any ridges that have air tumbling over and dropping down toward the canyon floor. **The route you pick should be across the canyon, away from the downdrafts on the upwind side.**

If you get caught in a downdraft, turn directly away from the mountain creating the turbulent wind. Remember on the other side of the canyon, the wind will start to climb back up the ridge.

A good visual scan of the runway is imperative before landing. Elk, deer, and once in awhile a monstrous moose will hide along the edges of the runway and try to run across the path of an approaching airplane. Keep your eyes scanning the runway and the timber next to the landing spot. Be ready to add power if you need to make a go-around.

You want to see any animals before you are in the flair part of the approach. If the wind is blowing and the ride rough, going around might not be a option near the ground. So keep your eyes scanning for any unseen hazards.

If you're the first pilot of the day to land on a backcountry airstrip, it is common practice to **fly down the runway**, hoping to scare off any unseen animals. This plan doesn't always work, animals get used to the airplanes and refuse to move. So, be careful. Hitting one of these animals will ruin a good vacation.

Your approach probably won't be the standard approach you learned during primary training. It might be a high right downwind to a short full-flap landing, or an in-close left downwind to a base turn at the end of the runway with a 100 foot turn to a landing.

**The time to practice these unorthodox approaches and landings is before you get into the mountains.**

All pilots should practice, practice, practice landings until he/she is skilled enough to land within **50 feet of any given spot**. Not once, but every time, and using different approaches to a landing.

Airspeed control is the key to landing on a spot. It doesn't do any good to dive down to the runway, gain excessive speed, and then float to the other end.

Touch down should be near stall speed. It also doesn't do any good to slam onto a runway at high speed and then slip and slide to the other end. **Mountain airstrips can be as slippery as ice after a rain shower.** Believe me when I say, "You will wish you had practiced spot landings as you slide toward the end of a runway."

Most landings in the mountains will be at a higher altitude than you are accustomed to. Because of the altitude gain, your airspeed will read off slightly, **but not enough to worry about**. Make the approach and landing the same as you practiced.

As the plane descends below the treetops, be ready to apply full power at the first sign of unanticipated wind. **Wind rolling over the trees can create abrupt wind shear or dead air that can make the wings lose lift. If this happens, the plane will drop like a rock.** Power is the only thing that will stop the rate of descent. More than one mountain pilot has had to apply full power to keep from slamming into the ground and still hit hard. **Power is your friend; always be ready to use it.**

Some runways can get real rough from animals digging in them. If you are flying a nose wheel airplane, you must make a soft field landing with the nose wheel off the ground. The main gear can handle the rough conditions, **but a nose wheel might come apart.**

I had a pilot make a landing at Shafer Meadows who told me that as I taxied up behind him he heard a loud clunk when the nose wheel touched down. Close examination revealed that he had broken the scissors that hold the wheel in place from falling out of its attachment.

He had lowered the front wheel to the ground right on top of a gopher hole. If he had taken off with the broken nose gear, it would have fallen off the plane. He would have realized he had a problem when the prop hit the ground during the next landing.

When you get the airplane stopped, taxi back to the tie-down area by **taxiing on the runway.** Do not taxi across the field--stay on the runway. Even though it might look smooth, the only area you can be confident in is the runway--use it. Many a prop has been bent by pilots who got in a hurry. If you inadvertently put a bend in your prop, wait for help. Don't try flying the plane with a bent prop.

Another pilot landed at Shafer Meadows Airstrip a couple of years ago. A whitetail deer raced ahead of the plane and veered to cross in front of the plane. The pilot saw the deer at the last second, but it was too late. The head of the deer hit the left horizontal stabilizer, right in the middle, and at the leading edge. The pilot hardly felt the deer hit and was shocked to see that the stabilizer was bent in past the spar. A rebuilt stabilizer was delivered and installed. It was hard to believe how much damage a little deer did to the plane. Imagine what a 1000-pound moose would do.

The airstrip to the left is Cayuse Airstrip in northern Idaho. It is down in the bottom of a deep canyon at 3000-foot elevation. The strip is a short 1800 feet long. The sectional map shows it as restricted. On a hot summer day the little runway can be very difficult to land on and depart from.

A high over-flight confirms the wind is out of the southwest. A left turn puts the plane on a downwind to the southwest approach. A sharp left descending turn brings the plane on final approach at about a quarter mile out. At this point, you need to slow down to the slowest possible speed for the short runway.

The snow on the airstrip had just melted leaving a water-filled and muddy runway. As I touched down I added power to help hold the nose of the plane up. The nose-high attitude and power would help move the plane through any soft spots that I might encounter.

The touchdown was smooth without any difficulties. I taxied to the south end and shut down. Mine was the first plane to land at this airstrip in the spring. The nearest person was probably 30 miles away. The only way to experience such an isolated sight is by flying to a mountain airstrip.

Following every back-country landing is a takeoff or departure. Taking off can be a lot more difficult than landing. You need to answer a few questions before you do. **Does my plane have enough power to take off at the high altitude?** What is the density altitude? What kind of wind will I encounter on the climb out? What is the best route to climb from ground level to altitude?

Unless you have a lot of mountain flying experience, it is best to **leave early before the heat of the day** raises the temperature, and the high mountain winds settle down into the canyons. The other option I don't recommend: depart an hour or so before dark. The wind will usually settle down later in the day, but the temperature won't change a lot. So, density altitude will still be high.

If you're flying a low-powered aircraft, you need to know for sure it will be able to get into the air when the density altitude is high. If any questions arise as to the outcome of a summer mountain takeoff, **wait for cooler conditions**. When the temperature cools down right before dark is an option, but remember that a late afternoon departure means that in case of an emergency landing most likely no will be looking for you until morning.

It is impossible to open a flight plan in the backcountry, but if possible, **leave a flight plan with anyone** else that is on the ground. Let them know where you are going to be and what route you plan to take. If you have other pilots camping nearby, give them your flight plan, or better yet find out when they're leaving and **fly out of the backcountry together**.

Having two planes on the same vacation will give you some added safety. Some backcountry airstrips have a ranger station with radios. Ask if you can use the radio, and file your flight plan and open it while you have the controller on the line. If for some reason you don't depart, call him back at let him know what you're doing.

**One of the most important items you could take on a wilderness vacation would be a satellite phone.** You will be able to make a call out anytime you want. The one problem with a satellite phone is the cost. But the money spent on a phone will be well worth it and might be one of a pilot's wisest purchases.

Most backcountry airstrips are at high elevations, which make the aircraft's performance diminish. Then add high temperatures that increase density altitude and you have the makings of a disaster if you don't take precautions. If temperatures are high, you need to make sure the plane you're flying can get into the air. **As temperatures increase during the day, density altitudes can soar to 8000 or 9000 feet.**

Check the operations manual for takeoff distance. Add a few hundred feet for grass and a hundred feet more for rough ground conditions. Once you have confirmed that the plane can get into the air, start the engine, and taxi all the way to the end of the runway. Be gentle with the power--**any abrupt power surges could pull rocks up into the propeller.** Taxi around any holes and turn around at the very end of the runway. Use the entire runway available.

Do your run-up over a spot that does not have any loose rocks. If the runway is real rocky, it might save a ding in the blades by checking the magnetos while you are taxiing. Keep your eyes outside while checking the mags; **you don't want to taxi into a hole and stick the prop into the ground.**

 Lean the engine for maximum power, but don't over-lean; using full power will create leaner conditions. When the plane gets airborne, enrich the mixture slightly. **Too lean of a mixture could damage an engine.**

Now is the point where you have to make a go, no-go decision. If it's a go, then think out the takeoff and be ready for an emergency. Pick a spot on the runway that will give you time to pull the power off and still get stopped. **If you haven't lifted off by the time you reach that spot, stop the takeoff attempt.** Taxi back to the tie-down area, and wait for better conditions, which might not come until the next morning.

Remember, never get in a hurry to get anywhere while flying in the mountains. Rule No. 5, never get into a hurry to get anywhere, would apply here.

Use all available power. Before you are committed to climb out, make sure the engine is producing maximum power.

As the plane climbs through five feet elevation, slowly relax the back pressure, and **level off over the runway.** Even though the aircraft is in the air, your takeoff and climb out is far from over.

You don't want to climb out of ground effect. Let the speed climb at the five feet elevation until you are nearly to the end of the runway. If you have 20 degrees of flaps, it will help to gain airspeed if you milk the flaps up to ten degrees. As the 10 degrees of flaps retract, the plane will settle slightly. Adjust elevator pressure to keep the plane from descending or ballooning. **The idea is to stay in ground effect, and to gain airspeed.**

As the end of the runway comes up, a slight back pressure will put the plane into a climb attitude. The higher airspeed gained while being in ground effect and level flight, combined with full power, **creates extra energy. Additional energy will give you extra power to climb out through any turbulence or downdrafts you may encounter.**

If you climb out at best rate speed, as recommended in most manufacturer's manuals, and hit a violent downdraft, you won't have any extra energy to give you another option. But one thing for sure, with slow airspeed you will descend toward the trees in the downdraft.

The additional airspeed will propel the plane through the turbulence and get you on your planned flight path. If you planned the right route to the up-air, the aircraft will climb easier to altitude. Somewhere above the mountains the air should smooth out. Then you can make your radio calls, and follow your planned route out of the mountains. After departing the airstrip and climbing to altitude, call Center or Flight Watch and let them know who you are, your location, and where you are going. Chances are you won't be able to contact anyone, but it's worth the piece of mind to make the effort.

There are times in the mountains when turbulence is everywhere. You still use the same technique: **fly the updraft ridges,** slow the plane to maneuvering speed, keep the wing as level as possible, and hang on for a rough ride. Though turbulence will probably not cause your plane to come apart, it could bend some parts. **If you get light in your seat** while experiencing turbulence, it's time to land and wait for a better day.

Not all airstrips in the mountains are level. You as the pilot need to know how to land on sloped runways. At times the wind may dictate an uphill takeoff or downhill landing. But don't let the wind direction help you make a mistake. When the wind is blowing strong, it might be possible to take off uphill, but one word of advice before you attempt an uphill takeoff: **don't do it.** Just a small uphill slope can lengthen a takeoff roll to the point that you won't get in the air, or when landing downhill, the down-slope will make stopping impossible. Unless you have a high horse-powered aircraft with a high rate of climb, wait for better conditions.

The pilot of a Piper Tri Pacer attempted a downhill landing on Meadow Creek airstrip in western Montana. The small plane floated down the runway, and finally touched down past the halfway point. The pilot braked hard, but realized that the end of the runway with a vertical cliff was approaching too fast. With 100 yards left, he added power for an attempted take-  off. The plane staggered into the air as the end of the runway passed under the plane.

The pilot relaxed when he realized that he was airborne, but his relaxation was premature. The left wheel hit a juniper bush, in the picture above, as the plane left the ground. The drag created from the contact slowed the plane, which in turn caused the plane to settle.

The plane slammed into a 100-foot high tree 60 feet from the ground and came to a sudden stop. As the plane slid down the tree, both passengers twisted with the airframe as it hit the ground.

The FAA called me the next day since the rescue crew had forgotten to shut off the emergency locator transmitter (ELT). To my surprise, it was impossible to recognize the aircraft. The plane was so badly damaged that I had to kick a hole in the side of the fuselage to find the ELT. Thankfully, both passengers survived the wreck, but not without broken bones.

The fifteenth *Rule to Live By*: IF A WILDERNESS AIR-STRIP HAS A SLOPE, ALWAYS LAND UPHILL AND TAKE OFF DOWNHILL.

**The sixteenth *Rule to Live By*: BEFORE ATTEMPTING A LANDING OR TAKEOFF, KNOW ALL FLIGHT CHARACTERISTICS OF THE AIRCRAFT YOU ARE FLYING.**

**The seventeenth *Rule to Live By*: STAY IN GROUND EFFECT DURING TAKEOFF TO BUILD EXTRA ENERGY. THIS ENERGY COULD SAVE YOUR LIFE.**

Years back I was flying rafting gear into a backcountry airstrip. The elevation was 5000 feet, with temperatures in the 90's. The Cessna 206 struggled with the density altitude and light turbulence, but it was flyable.

After my second landing, a pilot approached me and asked what I thought about he and his daughter departing in their Cessna 172. I replied he should wait until right before dark, or smarter yet, wait until morning when the temperature would be in the 50's.

I could tell by his expression he didn't like my answer. On the next landing he asked again what I thought of him taking off. My answer didn't change.

As I approached the small runway on the next flight, a rescue helicopter was taking off. I was shocked to hear **the pilot had tried a takeoff uphill** and then turned left toward rising terrain. The small Cessna staggered through the top of the trees and then plunged to the ground. The pilot and passenger survived.

It's hard to figure out what he was thinking. He had done all the wrong things by taking off in the heat of the day and attempting an uphill takeoff in an underpowered aircraft. Why was he willing to take such a risk? Both of them luckily survived. But it cost them a long stay in the hospital.

He broke a couple of *Rules to Live By*: No. 5, get-homeitis could get you killed. and No. 2, if caution isn't used, people will get hurt.

**Never risk life and limb while flying in the mountains.** If your time frame is limited, postpone your mountain trip until time isn't an issue.

CHAPTER 7 QUESTIONS:

1.  Will the wind a pilot finds at altitude be the same direction on the ground? _____

2.  Why does a mountain pilot stay over or close to the runway when letting down? _____

3.  Why is it important to check the runway out before landing?

    _____

4.  When is the time to practice non-standard approaches? _____

    _____

5.  What is the key to landing on a given spot? _____

    _____

6.  When encountering abrupt wind shear, what should a pilot do?

    _____

7.  Why is power your friend? _____

    _____

8.  Is it OK to straighten out a bent prop and then fly? Why? _____

    _____

9.  Why would a mountain pilot use a nose-high landing with a lot of power? _____

    _____

10. What questions need to be answered before departing a mountain airstrip? _____

    _____

11. What can a mountain pilot do to make his flight out of the backcountry safer? _____

    _____

12. What would be one of the most important things to take on a wilderness vacation? _____

13. What happens to density altitude as temperatures climb? _____

    _____

14. Why does a mountain pilot stay in ground effect while taking off?

    _____

15. If while flying in the mountains the turbulence is bad enough to make you light in the seat, what should you do? _____

    _____

16. When can a mountain pilot take off uphill? _____

    _____

# CHAPTER 8:

# UNIMPROVED RUNWAYS & OFF-AIRPORT LANDINGS

I used the airstrip above while working in Alaska. The airstrip was 900-feet long, narrow as the tires, full of brush and horribly muddy when it rained. The short runway had a hump in the middle that made it impossible for a pilot to see the other end of the runway until he rolled over the hump. The gravel airstrip ended at a small pond. Any mistake on the takeoff meant you would have an unwanted bath.

No pilot should attempt this type of airstrip unless you have the appropriate training and the right kind of airplane. This airstrip leaves no room for bad judgment.

While waiting for passengers at this airstrip I watched two Super Cubs attempt a landing. The runway was covered in mud, and the wind was gusting across the runway at 20 knots. One plane ended up on its back and the other one in pucker brush with a bent prop. Both pilots had recently bought the shiny new planes and had flown up from the lower forty-eight on vacation. This was their first landing on an unapproved airstrip. Their attempted landings proved both pilots needed specialized training on landing under those poor conditions.

As a mountain pilot, you must be able to judge a landing spot and be truthful about your abilities to land. Don't get in over your head and end up in an accident. It's not worth it.

If you are flying into a backcountry airstrip, **talk to local pilots about the best way to fly in and the techniques they use at the airstrip.** They've had years of experience and will be happy to help out a fellow pilot. A few words of advice could save you a lot of headache.

 An airplane, like the Super Cub at the left, has a tall gear, 31-inch tires, a bore prop, and requires a qualified pilot. It needs only a couple of hundred feet to land and take off safely.

The big tires only have a few pounds of air in them, so they can roll over a ten-inch log or grapefruit-sized rocks without any problems. The extended wings make it possible to land and take off at lower speeds than most planes.

This type of airplane will allow you to fly into many new places. *But remember that the pilot's ability must equal or exceed the capability of the airplane he's flying,* so training is essential before landing in wilderness environments with short-field takeoffs and landings.

**The eighteenth *Rule to Live By:* ONLY ATTEMPT A LANDING AT AIRSTRIPS WHERE THE PILOT AND AIRCRAFT ARE CAPABLE OF LANDING.**

The next picture shows an abandoned airstrip in the wilderness. *If possible, find a local pilot who is knowledgeable about emergency landing strips in the area and mark them on your map.* Then plan your flight to fly close to these emergency landing spots. These old airstrips are plentiful and make emergency landings possible.

Mechanical problems could occur during your mountain flight, so the following question should be foremost in your mind: What will I do if the engine quits? The first thing to do is to determine the problem. Most of the time it is one of two things: carburetor ice or fuel starvation.

Switching the tanks, full rich mixture, or carburetor heat will usually fix the problem. You must get the engine restarted immediately.

Knowing your emergency procedures and performing them accurately could make the difference between a successful emergency landing or not. Many pilots have wrecked planes because they did not switch the fuel indicator to the fullest tank. If nothing has changed after you have completed the emergency procedures, you must make a commitment to an emergency landing. **Make the commitment to the emergency landing while you still have enough time and altitude to find the best spot.**

At the first sign of an emergency, you should immediately trim for your best glide speed and turn toward the best possible landing area. During an emergency you will see the importance of maintaining higher altitude when flying in the mountains. Because of altitude, a pilot has time to scan the landscape and find the best possible place to attempt a landing.

Is the river in the picture at the left a good spot? Although it does have areas devoid of trees, the big boulders in the water would make it a metal-bending landing spot.

The gravel bar at the bottom right of the photo has smaller rocks and looks fairly flat. If this type of flat gravel bar is available, **it might be your best bet to survive a landing.** If you are going to attempt a landing on a gravel bar, it needs to be a minimum of 400 feet in length. Expect that the plane probably won't stay on the wheels. **It will probably flip on its back.**

The issue you need to concern yourself with is getting down on the very small gravel bar at minimal airspeed. Most likely, you would slide off the end and into the trees at the other end, but a mountain pilot should be willing to slide off the end of an emergency landing spot at 30 miles an hour. At that speed, surviving is highly likely.

One mistake a pilot cannot afford to make is to ignore the airspeed. If you are going too fast when you get down to the gravel bar, you will fly over it or bounce off the bar and slam into the boulder-filled river just past the bar. Your chance of surviving such a landing would be slim. This is the reason for practicing power-off landings to a designated spot. Practice until you can land on that spot every time--not just once in awhile. **The time to practice emergency landings is when the engine is working.** Every time you land your airplane, force yourself to practice emergency landings. *Stay emergency conscious all the time.*

The shoreline on the picture at the left is possibly an emergency landing spot, but upon closer examination you will notice the shoreline has a steep grade and is covered with 3-foot high stumps.

Trying to land on the water between the shoreline and the ice is probably not a good choice. Although it looks inviting, the ice hasn't totally melted, so the water is probably about 35 degrees. You also see snow on the shoreline, which means that the outside air temperature must be near freezing. Surviving a landing in the water between the shoreline and the ice is possible, but it doesn't mean that you would survive being wet in cold conditions once you got out of the water.

Landing on the ice and then breaking through and sinking would be a death trap. This is an island, which means you are stuck on it and can't leave to get help. Using this emergency landing spot would not be a good choice.

After a pilot has made a decision to make an emergency landing and has picked a likely spot, he has to figure out the route of flight that will get him and his passengers down to the intended landing spot. The touchdown has to be made at the slowest possible speed with the nose up and under control. Remember the passengers are in the cabin. Use the landing gear and the wings to absorb the impact – **not the cabin.**

The fourth rule would come into play here: In an emergency, fly the aircraft and maintain control all the way to the ground. **Having control is the difference between surviving or not.**

If time permits while your altitude is high and after you have picked your emergency landing spot, do your emergency check again -- *but don't get distracted.* The initial shock of having an engine grind to a stop might cause a pilot to forget an item. Once you have made the commitment and turn toward your selected spot, perform the emergency check one more time. If you missed an item, hopefully you will catch it the second time around.

Anytime you are flying in the mountains you should be listening to Center or Flight Watch frequencies, which can be received almost everywhere in the United States if your plane is high enough. If you have these agency frequencies tuned in your radio, you will be able to declare an emergency by just keying the mike. If you have to make an emergency call, in your calmest voice tell them what emergency problems you are having and your best estimate of your location. **But don't get distracted from what is going to happen, an emergency landing.**

It would be smart to call one of these agencies before you enter the mountains and tell them what you are doing, where you are going, and when you are returning. Take the time to give them your expected route of flight, too. If they have to look for you, they will know where to start the search.

**Flying as high as possible while in the mountains** will give a pilot an added advantage. The altitude will give you more time to find the best available landing spot and also make it possible to call for help at the first sign of a problem.

**The nineteenth *Rule to Live By*: WHEN WEATHER PERMITS, FLY TWO THOUSAND FEET ABOVE THE MOUNTAINS.**

If everything has gone according to plan, and you have been able to land the aircraft on the emergency landing spot, it's time to get out of the plane and take care of any injured passengers. **Having a hand-held radio is very important.** Make your emergency calls on 121.5. Airliners and government agencies monitor this frequency. It shouldn't take long before you get someone to answer your calls.

Your aircraft is equipped with an ELT. Some airplanes have a switch on the dash to activate the device, others have to be activated on the unit itself. Turn the switch to activate. It would also be wise to have a spare pocket-sized ELT. Carry the spare one in your shirt pocket and **activate it at the first sign of a problem.** If for some reason the ELT in the plane doesn't work correctly, **the spare one will bring help.**

If you didn't have time to make an emergency call and haven't heard any reply from your hand-held radio calls, you will be glad to know satellites pass a couple of times a day. They will pick up your ELT signals and call in your location to the local Search and Rescue. Help should be there shortly. **Don't leave the plane, unless it is a short walk for help.** If you leave the plane, leave a message with directions where you went.

A Cessna 206 crash-landed in The Great Bear Wilderness. The two surviving passengers were slightly injured and stayed at the wreckage overnight. They could see helicopters hunting for them low in the valley below, but the weather was snowy and cold, so they decided to leave the plane and hike to safety. The wreckage was found the next morning, but with no apparent sign of survivors. The plane had burned so completely it was impossible to say for sure how many bodies were inside the burned-out plane. Because of the severity of the wreck, the rescue was called off.

The two surviving passengers found the highway a day after the search had been called off. In this case, the passengers probably saved their own lives, but remember: *If you do leave a wrecked plane, make sure you leave a message stating who you are and where you are going.*

The picture to the right shows a small, shallow lake surrounded by a heavily treed area. The lake has marshland with brush on the right side. If you land in the water, it needs to be close to the shoreline.

When an airplane lands in water, **it will sink within a minute**, so if you decide to attempt a water landing, you must get out of the plane immediately. If you accidentally hit your head and become impaired in any way, chances are good you would sink with the plane.

**Open the doors and windows if time permits.** If the airplane's cabin is bent, the doors may possibly jam shut. If you get out of the plane and swim to shore, you have another problem -- getting dry and making a shelter. **Landing on the lake would be a last resort, but a better choice than landing in tall trees.**

The picture on the left shows an unimproved logging road. Along each side is dirt and brush plowed into piles. The road is short, but it is possible to make a survivable landing. The best bet would be to land on the lower end of the road going uphill. You may hit the dirt banks at the curve, but at 30 miles per hour the landing is survivable. **Remember to open the doors,** if you can, turn the fuel off, and touch down at the slowest possible speed.

Remove pens and pencils from your front shirt pockets and tighten your shoulder harness. If time permits have the front seat passenger get in the back seat. That would move the center of gravity aft and help the pilot get the nose up and tail down for a slower approach and shorter ground roll.

The picture to the right shows a road running through heavy timber. The road is straight, with plenty of length. The first question to be answered is, "Is the road width wide enough for the wings?" One clue would be **if the road is paved**, which would mean the width is adequate for the wings. **If the road was graveled,** you probably wouldn't have enough clearance between the wings and the trees.

Signs along the side of the road are always a hazard, but this would be a good emergency landing spot. Circling over the top of the road would give the pilot a good look at the touchdown area.

Look for any power lines crossing the highway, and concentrate on staying directly above the centerline of the highway. Land as slow as possible to make the roll-out short with less chance of hitting objects alongside the road. As you float down past the trees, concentrate on being dead center over the road. Try to ignore the closeness of the trees and keep an eye out for power lines. Make a full stall landing and brake hard to a stop. The chance of making a successful landing on a highway is excellent.

The picture below shows high mountains. The top fourth is bare of vegetation, leaving solid granite rock. The lower three-quarters is covered with heavy timber, and brush-filled draws, or slides, between the ridges. Even though the steep-sloped mountainside doesn't look like a good place to attempt a landing, there is a possible spot. But this would be the last choice, and only if there are no lakes, meadows, open areas, or gravel bars available.

Attempting an emergency landing anywhere in the large timber on the hillside is out of the question. The timber will tear the plane apart before you fall to the ground, making a survival highly unlikely. Hoping to land between large trees so the wings will absorb the impact is unrealistic. You have a better option for landing in the trees, which we will discuss later.

The brush-filled draw, between the stands of trees, is the only spot to make a survivable attempt. Under the brush is a thin layer of dirt and then solid rock. Although this may sound like a hard landing and not very encouraging, we don't plan to slam into the draw. Once you have made the decision to make an emergency landing on this hillside the question remains, how can a pilot make a reasonable landing in this area and survive?

Before we go into details, let me repeat this spot should only be attempted if **nothing else exists.**

Making this decision will not be easy, but the decision must be made while you still have enough altitude to complete the attempt. The pilot would need to **dive to gain speed** and then use that speed to climb up the draw. *If the approach is started too slow or too low, the plane will not have enough momentum to stop the dive, level out, and climb up the draw.* To make this landing possible, a pilot will need to build extra energy or speed in the dive, then level the plane and climb uphill with the remaining energy.

As the plane's airspeed decreases -- which will be quick -- the pilot needs to be in the draw, settling toward the brush (or ground) as the plane slows to near stall speed. The ideal situation is to impact the ground nose up and as slowly as possible. Hopefully the plane will settle onto the ground gently and come to a stop in a few feet.

One problem with this type of emergency landing is there is no way to practice it. But let me say it again, this would be a last possible spot to pick and should only be attempted if nowhere else exists. None theless, this could be survivable.

The picture to the right shows a high mountain valley with nothing but timber below. An engine loss there would mean attempting an emergency landing in the timber, which is not a pleasant thought. If landing in the trees is your only option, then you need to commit to the decision and figure out what plan  would provide your best chance for survival. Make sure the wings and gear take the punishment by absorbing the initial impact.

Some of the worst advice pilots have been told regarding this type of emergency is to fly the plane into the trees with the fuselage between trees stumps, and let the wings take the impact. This type of emergency landing **should never be attempted**. After the wings have been torn off the plane and fuel begins running into the fuselage, your survival rate would be unbelievably low.

There is a better option. A pilot should find the thickest stand of trees and **try to float into the top of the trees with a nose-high attitude flying as slowly as possible.** Your flaps should be full down, fuel shut off, and seat belts tightened. The theory behind this maneuver is that the thick, young-growth timber will cushion the impact and bring the plane to a stop without a lot of damage to the fuselage. This type of emergency landing would give you a far better chance of surviving.

Lodge pole pine is the type of tree growing in an area after a forest fire has burned through it. **They grow in thick groves** – sometimes so thick it is impossible to walk through them. They aren't very tall, and **they are usually lighter in color** than the old-growth timber.

From the air, you will be able to see where forest fires have burned through timber stands. If no other choices are available, and an emergency landing in the trees is your only option, pick out the new-growth timber and make a nose-up, slow-speed landing onto the top of a stand of trees. **We hope the thickness of the timber will cushion the plane** as it comes to a stop and the trees will hold up the plane, or bend enough to let the plane settle to the ground.

Although this type of emergency doesn't sound survivable, these techniques are better options than slamming into the ground at high-speed or ramming into large tree stumps.

As I mentioned earlier, you must be able to land on a spot, at the slowest possible speed to have any chance of surviving. Rule to Live By No. 4, maintain control all the way to the ground, would apply here.

The picture to the left shows a frozen mountain lake with snow on top of the ice. If the snow isn't deeper than a foot, you might be able to touch down and remain on the wheels. **If the snow is crusted, the plane wheels might dig into the snow** and possibly flip the plane on its back. If this is where you have committed to land, a soft field, nose-up landing would be your best choice.

Because the lake is long enough, you should get the plane in ground effect and as the plane gets closer to the ice increase the angle of attack until the wheels touch the snow. If the plane has a retractable landing gear, leave the gear up, and let the plane slide to a stop like a sled.

Then you have the problem of waiting for help. Rule No. 1 would come into effect here. Be prepared. Always have your survival gear handy and full of the equipment to make your stay comfortable.

The picture below shows a meadow mostly full of water. A good emergency landing spot is located along the tree line and in the grass,

but did you notice the frost in the shadow of the trees where the sun hasn't hit? This should tell you the air temperature is cold -- making for cold nights and cool days. You could survive the landing only to suffer from hypothermia because you are not prepared to survive a few days in cold weather.

If you landed in a spot like this, the wheels of the plane would dig into the sod of the meadow, and most likely flip the plane on its back. If that happens, the doors will jam when the fuselage is bent, leaving you trapped in the cabin. So open the doors prior to landing. If you are flying a retract aircraft, leaving the gear up would probably keep the plane from flipping. Remember, airspeed control and the ability to land on a spot are the keys to making a successful emergency landing.

"Emergency landing" is something most pilots will never have to say while they are flying. But if by chance the engine quits and won't restart, remember the following:

1. All pilots should be proficient in all emergency procedures. Don't just have the procedure memorized -- know what each item does.

2. A mountain pilot must be able to perform non-standard approaches and departures, and must be able to land at a selected spot every time.

3. A mountain pilot should always be scanning the ground around the plane making mental notes about possible landing spots.

4. A mountain pilot will never fly into adverse weather conditions beyond his ability.

## CHAPTER 8 QUESTIONS:

1. What is eighteenth *Rule to Live By*? _____
   _____

2. Why would it be smart to talk to local pilots about wilderness airstrips? _____

3. Why would an abandoned airstrip in the mountains be important to a mountain pilot? _____

4. What question should always be on a mountain pilot's mind? _____
   _____

5. Why does a mountain pilot fly at higher altitudes when possible?
   _____

6. Why does a mountain pilot have to make a commitment to an emergency landing? _____
   _____

7. What is meant by emergency current? _____
   _____

8. Why would it be smart to call the Flight Service before entering the mountains? _____
   _____

9. Why would a mountain pilot have Flight Service or Center frequencies tuned to the airplane's radio while in the mountains? _____
   _____

10. What is the nineteenth *Rule to Live By* and what is its importance?
    _____
    _____

11. Why would a mountain pilot carry an extra ELT with him? _____
    _____

12. When making an emergency landing in water, how long will the plane float? _____

13. Why would a pilot open the doors and windows before attempting an emergency landing in water? _____
    _____

14. If time permits why would a front seat passenger climb into the back seat? _____

15. When landing on a frozen lake, what technique would a pilot use?
    _____
    _____

16. When talking about emergency landings, what four items must a mountain pilot be proficient in? _____

_____

_____

_____

_____

_____

# Chapter 9:

# Emergency Survival Gear

What survival gear should a mountain pilot carry in the plane? That particular question has already been answered in many ways. A pilot should always plan for the unexpected. If pilots do their homework, we hope in the case of an emergency landing, Search and Rescue will be at the wreck site within a few hours.

However, if no one knew where you are heading or when to expect you back, no one will begin hunting for your downed airplane. In this unfortunate situation, a pilot better have the right survival gear.

It's a fact that most of the time a pilot gets out of a wrecked airplane with only what he is wearing. The survival gear could burn up in the plane. One thing a pilot can do is to wear a **survival vest** with a lot of pockets filled with gear. Then when the pilot exits the plane, he takes his important survival gear with him. Wearing a survival vest in the heat of summer will be a little uncomfortable but having the gear with you all the time is paramount. So, **buy a vest and fill it full of your gear**: your extra ELT, handheld radio, plastic bags, matches, and first aid kit. It will be worth the effort.

Without the right gear, the rate of survival drops drastically. **Having the right survival gear while flying in the mountains is as**

**important as having enough gasoline in the plane.** What you are doing is investing in your and your family's future.

Being found as soon as possible is the top priority. The following items are what I recommend for survival gear. Add items to your liking. The more you have, the more comfortable your unexpected stay will be.

1.  Handheld radio with extra batteries. Calls can be made in the blind on the emergency frequency, 121.5. Airlines and other mountain pilots monitor this frequency.
2.  Satellite phone. Calls can be made for help immediately after departing a downed aircraft.
3.  Pocket-sized ELT. Turn the ELT on the second you know you are going to make an emergency landing, not after you land.
4.  Tent or tarps. Getting out of the weather by pitching a tent or covering up with a tarp can stop the onset of hypothermia.
5.  Sleeping bags. The waterproof type if possible, and one for each passenger.
6.  First aid kit. All items found in any industrial kit.
7.  Water. If weight permits take water and a container to haul water. Not always possible
8.  Flashlights, with extra batteries, and candles.
9.  Food. Enough for a three day's supply for each passenger.
10. Signal flare, flashing beacons, or flare gun.
11. Waterproof matches with fire starter.
12. Large garbage bags or rain gear.
13. Extra cold weather clothing: stocking cap, gloves, coats, stockings and winter boots.
14. Cooking pot for heating water.
15. Knife, shovel, ax, or hatchet.
16. Nylon rope, insect repellant, head net.
17. Snow shoes in winter.
18. Signal mirror and fish hooks.
19. Rifle or handgun. This item is optional.
20. Duct tape. This should probably be near the top of the list. It has a million uses.

The survival equipment you bring should be what you are comfortable with. The list above is the minimum. The first aid kit should be in a dust-proof and moisture-proof metal or heavy plastic container. The first aid kit should be readily accessible to the pilot and passengers. The contents should include the following minimum items:

1. Adhesive bandage compresses (3 inches long).
2. Antiseptic or alcohol wipes.
3. Bandage compresses.
4. Triangular bandage compresses, 40 inches long.
5. Roller bandages, 4 inch by 5 yards.
6. Adhesive tape, 1 inch by 5 yards.
7. Bandage scissors.
8. Bandages.
9. Pain pills--optional.
10. Sutures--optional.
11. Splint material--optional.

CHAPTER 9 QUESTIONS:

1. A mountain pilot should always prepare for what? Explain.

   _____

2. When buying survival gear, what is a pilot investing in?

   _____

3. Why is wearing a survival vest so important? _____

   _____

4. Why is a satellite phone or handheld radio important? _____

   _____

5. What is the emergency frequency for your handheld radio?

   _____

# CHAPTER 10:

# MOUNTAIN FLYING
## AIRPLANES

**One deciding factor to help a pilot make a go, no-go decision is what type of airplane he is flying.** A Cessna 150 doesn't have any extra power to compensate for a downdraft whereas a Cessna 185 has an abundance of extra power to help defeat a downdraft. But sometimes it doesn't matter how much extra power is available. **Mother Nature is unpredictable.**

Mountain flying can be an exacting challenge that takes practice, caution, and the right frame of mind to perform with a degree of success. **But all pilots can learn the techniques**, and with some practical experience, feel safe in the mountains.

All pilots can learn to navigate the mountains successfully. The one item left to debate is what type of aircraft can be flown in the mountains with a degree of safety.

Every airplane made can fly in mountains under the right conditions. The key words here are, "THE RIGHT CONDITIONS!"

On a perfect day, no wind, clear sky, a Cessna 150 can fly over 7000 to 10,000 foot peaks of the Rocky Mountains without any problems and land at a backcountry airstrip. As long as the pilot departs the high-altitude airstrip before the heat of the day, the underpowered plane will fly off with just a little effort.

CESSNA **150**

That same pilot of the Cessna 150 may accomplish the flight with just a little bit of worry and leave the airplane tied down at his local airport thinking flying in the mountains is a piece of cake. He also might think all the stories about the dangers of mountain flying are fabricated myths. After all, he was right when he hadn't listened to other mountain pilots' concerns about the Cessna 150. He had flown in the mountains with the small plane and returned his way without a problem.

But a day in turbulent winds -- winds at the mountain tops 30 knots or higher-- that same pilot would at the minimum scare the hell out of himself and at the maximum kill himself and his passengers. So, remember that **under the ideal conditions just about any airplane can fly in the mountains successfully.** But a day later the same plane and pilot might never return home.

**The twentieth** *Rule to Live By*: **ON A GOOD DAY A LOW-POWERED AIRPLANE CAN FLY IN THE MOUNTAINS, BUT ON A WINDY DAY, THE SAME PLANE MIGHT NOT BE ABLE TO HANDLE THE MOUNTAINS.**

## SUPER CUB

I have owned four Piper Super Cubs. They handle the mountains well, but I've also had a few problems with the venerable airplane. At high altitude the plane's power output drops to the point where the winds can be stronger than the plane's forward speed, leaving not enough fuel to get home. When this happened I'd have to retreat with the wind on my tail to wait out the weather and get more fuel. The cub's a great plane, but as for me -- *I like a lot of horsepower.*

Some low wing airplanes can handle mountain winds. Pipers, Bonanzas, Ralleys, and Mooney's are a few planes that visit the back-country airstrips often. The more horsepower the safer it gets. The low wings make for an easier landing but they also restrict downward visibility.

One of the best-known mountain planes is the Cherokee Six. It is the favorite of a lot of backcountry pilots and handles the job well.

## Cessna 185

Nearly all the Cessna's have proven they can handle the mountains. The 172 and the 150 are marginal airplanes, but if you are going into the mountains with either of these planes, I recommend you have a lot of experience or an experienced pilot with you.

The Cessna 210 has plenty of power to handle the mountains, but the retractable landing gear isn't nearly as tough as fixed gear, which makes damaging it more likely.

The Cessna 182, 180, 206 and 185 have made thousands of landings in the mountains and have proven they can handle the job. The high-winged airplanes work well, and in brushy conditions the wings stay up out of the brush.

Light twins can handle the longer mountain airstrips, but their props are lower to the ground making it a lot easier to ding a prop. They also have retractable gears that can be damaged. The approach speed of the twins is higher. Running off the end of a short mountain airstrip is more likely. A twin can handle the job, but extra care must be taken during landings and takeoffs.

The following chart details abilities of some airplanes in the mountains. A number from one to five will follow each aircraft. A rating of five is the best rating with one being the worst.

| Aircraft | Rating | Ability to Handle Mountain Winds and Altitudes | Precautions |
|---|---|---|---|
| Cessna 150-152 | 1 | Underpowered, questionable in the mountains | Experienced pilot required |
| Cessna 170 | 1 | Underpowered, questionable | Two seater aircraft, tail wheel |
| Cessna 172 | 2 | Can perform with caution | Two seater aircraft in the mountains |
| Cessna 177 | 2 | Poor mountain plane | Underpowered |
| Cessna 182 | 4 | Handles mountains well | Weak nose gear, land on mains |
| Cessna 180 | 4 | Handles mountains well | Tail wheel aircraft, can ground loop |
| Cessna 185 | 5 | Handles mountains well | Tail wheel aircraft, can ground loop |
| Cessna 206 | 5 | Good mountain plane | Plenty of power |
| Cessna 210 | 3 | Handles mountains | Retract gear, prop close to the ground |
| Piper Tomahawk | 1 | Underpowered, questionable | Experienced pilot required |
| Piper Cherokee 140 | 2 | Underpowered, questionable | Two seater aircraft |
| Piper Cherokee 180 | 3 | Can perform with caution | Check density altitude |

| | | | |
|---|---|---|---|
| Piper Comanche | 3 | Handles mountains | Retract, prop low to the ground |
| Piper Arrow | 2 | Handles mountains | Retract, two seater |
| Piper Cherokee Six | 4 | Handles mountains well | Prop low to the ground |
| Piper Tri Pacer | 1 | Can perform with caution | Two seater, early morning departure |
| Piper Pacer | 2 | Can perform with caution | Two seater, tail wheel aircraft |
| Piper Super Cub | 4 | Handles mountains | Tail wheel aircraft |
| Piper PA-11 | 2 | Underpowered, no-flaps | Tail wheel aircraft |
| Piper Warrior | 3 | Handles mountains | Two place airplane in the mountains |
| Mooney | 2 | Can perform with caution | Retract, prop is low to the ground |
| Bonanza | 2 | Handles mountains | Retract, prop is low to the ground |
| Aeronca | 2 | Can perform with caution | Tail wheel, early mornings |
| Citabria | 3 | Can handle mountains | Tail wheel, early mornings |
| Aviat Husky | 4 | Handles mountains | Tail wheel aircraft |
| Luscombe | 1 | Underpowered | Tail wheel, experienced pilot |
| Maule | 4 | Good mountain plane | Tail wheel |

| Ralley | 3 | Can handle mountains | Prop low to the ground |
|---|---|---|---|
| Helio Courier | 5 | Good mountain plane | Tail wheel |
| Mooney | 2 | Poor mountain plane | Nose wheel |

You can see from the above chart there are a lot of planes that fly in the mountains with some degree of safety. Just recently a lot of home-built, high-wing airplanes have come on the market. Most of them are lightweight, but have plenty of power. Because of the weight it would be wise to get in and out of the mountains early or late in the day. But a pilot's experience level is what really determines which planes perform well. The more experienced the pilot, the lower horse-powered plane he can fly.

A Mountain Pilot with his Super-Cub

# SUMMARY:

**You, as a pilot, are the only one to gauge your flying skills.** You know your aviation background, so be honest with yourself and your passengers about your mountain flying skills. Your passengers only know you have a license to fly an airplane. But having a pilot's license doesn't mean you have the ability to fly everywhere safely. So before leaving on your flight into the mountains, you owe it to yourself and your passengers to get as familiar as possible with the upcoming flight.

**You need to determine the airplane you are using can handle the demands of the mountains.** Anytime you are going to make a flight away from your home base have your mechanic check the points in the magnetos and clean the spark plugs. One bad spark plug could force you and your family to sit on a backcountry airstrip and wait for help. **Take the time to have the plane checked out by a certified mechanic.**

Two bankers were flying home from the eastern United States. Their home base was Polson, Montana. While on the arc of an instrument approach into Glacier Park International Airport, they disappeared off the controller's radar scope. The last known location was one mountain ridge from the Flathead Valley, only 10 minutes from home.

The search started at first light the next morning. Everyone knew they had to be just inside the mountains. It shouldn't have been a problem to find the plane. The search went on day after day and was finally called off when 700 hours of flight time didn't find the plane.

The father of one of the pilots hired me to continue searching for his son. I had recently finished a ten-year grizzly bear study in the same area. The wreck happened on April 11, and the bears come out of their dens about the first of May. The transmitting collar on one of the big male grizzlies led me to the crash site. A helicopter dropped me off on a rock where I bushwhacked through a mile of thick, cliffy area until I found the plane. The plane had slammed into a rock-face at a tremendous speed. Both passengers died on impact. The bears at the site had been cleaning up the remains, and they weren't going to give up the free food without a fight. I hastily departed with my shotgun ready.

The point I'm trying to make is an aircraft that has gone down in steep, brushy, and tree-covered mountains can be impossible to find. If these two men would have survived the wreck, they both would have starved to death or been killed by grizzly bears. The importance of preparing for a trip into the mountains can't be emphasized enough. Never fly beyond your abilities, and be prepared.

**Learning to fly in the mountains can be very rewarding. The Twenty *Rules To Live By* are guidelines to follow every time you are in the mountains.** Learn them, study them, and live by them. The sights and sounds in the mountains will be rewarding and well worth the extra effort.

## CHAPTER 10 AND SUMMARY QUESTIONS:

1. What factor does your airplane have on making a go, no-go decision? _____

2. Can a 'high time' mountain pilot fly in the mountains no matter what the conditions are? _____

3. What does it take to fly in the mountains? _____

4. What is the twentieth *Rule to Live By* and explain its meaning. ____
   _____

5. What is the one item in the mountains a pilot can never have enough of? _____

6. What really determines which planes perform well in the mountains?
   _____

7. Who can judge a pilot's flying abilities? _____

8. What do you owe your passengers before taking them in the mountains? _____

9. What can a bad spark plug do to your plane's performance?
   _____

10. What should you know before flying in the mountains?
    _____
    _____

# CHECKLIST: THE TWENTY *RULES TO LIVE BY*:

1.\_\_\_ BE PREPARED
2.\_\_\_ IF CAUTION ISN'T USED, PEOPLE CAN GET HURT
3.\_\_\_ WHEN POSSIBLE FLY THE SAFEST ROUTE, NOT THE FASTEST
4.\_\_\_ IN AN EMERGENCY, FLY THE AIRCRAFT AND MAINTAIN CONTROL ALL THE WAY TO THE GROUND. HAVING CONTROL IS THE DIFFERENCE IN SURVIVING OR NOT.
5.\_\_\_ NEVER GET INTO A HURRY TO GET ANYWHERE. GET-HOMEITIS KILLS PEOPLE
6.\_\_\_ ONCE YOU CHOOSE A SURVIVABLE LANDING SPOT, STICK WITH IT
7.\_\_\_ IF YOU HAVE A CHOICE, DON'T FLY OVER ROADLESS AREAS IN THE WINTER
8.\_\_\_ IF THE FORECASTED WIND AT THE MOUNTAIN TOPS IS 30 KNOTS -- STAY HOME
9.\_\_\_ FLY EARLY IN THE MORNING OR LATE IN THE EVENING
10.\_\_\_ UP-AIR IS GOOD, DOWN-AIR IS BAD
11.\_\_\_ WHEN ENTERING LOW FORWARD VISIBILITY, MAKE A 180 DEGREE TURN IMMEDIATELY
12.\_\_\_ NEVER FLY INTO FOG OR CLOUDS WHILE IN THE MOUNTAINS
13.\_\_\_ FLY UP ONE SIDE OF A CANYON, AND LEAVE PLENTY OF ROOM TO TURN AROUND
14.\_\_\_ NEVER FLY IN FREEZING RAIN
15.\_\_\_ IF A WILDERNESS AIRSTRIP HAS A SLOPE, ALWAYS LAND UPHILL AND TAKE OFF DOWNHILL
16.\_\_\_ BEFORE ATTEMPTING A LANDING OR TAKEOFF, KNOW ALL FLIGHT CHARACTERISTICS OF THE AIRCRAFT YOU ARE FLYING
17.\_\_\_ STAY IN GROUND EFFECT DURING TAKEOFF TO BUILD EXTRA ENERGY. THIS ENERGY COULD SAVE YOUR LIFE
18.\_\_\_ ONLY ATTEMPT A LANDING AT AIRSTRIPS WHERE THE PILOT AND AIRCRAFT ARE CAPABLE OF LANDING
19.\_\_\_ WHEN WEATHER PERMITS, FLY TWO THOUSAND FEET ABOVE THE MOUNTAINS
20.\_\_\_ ON A GOOD DAY A LOW-POWERED AIRPLANE CAN FLY IN THE MOUNTAINS, BUT ON A WINDY DAY, THE SAME PLANE MIGHT NOT BE ABLE TO HANDLE THE MOUNTAINS

# ABOUT THE AUTHOR

As a native of Montana, DAVID J. HOERNER was familiar with the backcountry long before he became a pilot. His boyhood home was just outside the border of Glacier National Park where he grew up hunting and fishing the backcountry of Montana, and he was a logger before learning to fly. He is now a commercial pilot with over 25,000 hours flying in Alaska and Montana. Dave is a Part 135 Chief Pilot, owns a Part 141 Flight School for airplanes, and provides helicopter instruction through his flight school. He is a CFII for airplanes, a helicopter intructor, and one of the few FAA certified pilot examiners for airplanes and helicopters in the United States. Over the years he has carried wolves and grizzly bears in his aircraft while doing some of his many flights for the US Forest Service and the Montana Department of Fish, Wildlife, and Parks. Dave has two children, Ryan and Bree, and resides in Kalispell, Montana. *Advanced Mountain Flying Techniques* is his second book; his first *Flying Alaska Gold: Grizzlies, Gold, Gangsters* is about his adventures as an inexperienced Alaskan bush pilot.

"I've spent a lot of time in the right seat of Dave Hoerner's Cessna 185 radio tracking lynx, coyotes, wolves, and wolverine over some of the most remote country in the lower 48. He is, quite simply, the finest pilot I've ever had the privilege to fly with. Not only does he fly as if the plane is an extension of himself, but he's got an intuitive sense of where the animals will be that's almost spooky. Over time, I've begun to realize that he is a great pilot because he has lived and flown through more than most people ever will. From working the gold fields in Alaska to flying the Montana wilderness, Dave Hoerner definitely has some stories to tell."
-- Jay Colby, USFS Wildlife Biologist

"From tracking grizzly bears on the highest peaks of Glacier National Park, to ferrying wolves from Canada to Yellowstone National Park, to locating fires in Montana's remote wilderness, Dave has done it all. For over ten years I have had the opportunity to fly with Dave on fire detection and wildlife survey flights, and I can truly say there is no better mountain pilot around."
-- Bill Michaels, Glacier National Park Fire Recon Specialist